# THE SIN OF CERTAINTY

# THE SIN
# OF CERTAINTY

WHY GOD DESIRES OUR TRUST
MORE THAN OUR "CORRECT" BELIEFS

## PETER ENNS

**HarperOne**
*An Imprint of HarperCollinsPublishers*

THE SIN OF CERTAINTY. Copyright © 2016 by Peter Enns. All rights reserved. Printed in the United
States of America. No part of this book may be used or reproduced in any manner whatsoever
without written permission except in the case of brief quotations embodied in critical articles and
reviews. For information, address HarperCollins Publishers, 195 Broadway, New York, NY 10007.

HarperCollins books may be purchased for educational, business, or sales promotional use.
For information, please email the Special Markets Department at SPsales@harpercollins.com.

FIRST HARPERCOLLINS PAPERBACK EDITION PUBLISHED IN 2017

*Designed by Terry McGrath*

Library of Congress Cataloging-in-Publication Data is available upon request.

ISBN 978–0–06–227209–6

23 24 25 26 27  LBC  13 12 11 10 9

*As always, and with love and thanks, to my family,
and to those who are weary and heavy-laden, seeking rest.*

Who among you fears the LORD and obeys the voice
of his servant, who walks in darkness and has no light, yet trusts
in the name of the LORD and relies upon his God?

—Isaiah 50:10


Trust in the LORD with all of your heart,
and do not rely on your own insight.

—Proverbs 3:5


As for knowledge, it will come to an end.
For we know only in part.

—1 Corinthians 13:8–9

# Contents

# I Don't Know What
# I Believe Anymore

My soul is full of troubles, and my life draws near to Sheol.

—Psalm 88:3

# Thanks for Nothing, Walt Disney

A few years ago, I was on my way home from a (boring, Lord-help-me-get-out-of-here) academic conference on the West Coast and thought it would be nice to chill with an onboard movie, which airlines used to offer before they gave up trying. Nothing looked remotely interesting except for Disney's film adaptation of *Bridge to Terabithia*, so . . . sure . . . why not, let's give it a shot. I can't recall my exact thought process, but I guess Disney's marketing assumption that your inner ten-year-old never really goes away is right on the money.

The movie tells the story of a friendship between two fifth graders in rural Virginia, Jess and his new neighbor, Leslie. Jess is a shy and self-conscious boy from a poor and fundamentalist Christian family. Leslie couldn't be more opposite—an a-religious free spirit with a contagious imagination, and who looks at life as one adventure after another. They become close friends, but Jess isn't always sure how to think about Leslie's nonconformist ideas.

In one scene, Jess and Leslie, along with Jess's spunky little sister May Belle, are in the back of the family pickup truck on the way home from church. Jess had invited Leslie, who seems to have spent her entire life insulated from the kind of world Jess takes for granted.

For Leslie going to church is another opportunity for an adventure into the unknown. She is glad she came along, despite the hellfire-and-brimstone preaching, and declares, "That whole Jesus thing. It's really interesting."

May Belle is absolutely shocked and corrects Leslie: "It's not interesting. It's scary. It's nailing holes through your hand. It's because we're all vile sinners that God made Jesus die."

Leslie looks at May Belle like she had just told her she believed babies were delivered by storks. "Do you really think that's true?"

Not only do they believe it, but Jess tells her they *have* to because "it's in the Bible." May Belle dutifully adds that if you don't believe in the Bible, "God will damn you to hell when you die."

Leslie will have none of it. "I seriously do *not* think God goes around damning people to hell. He's too busy running all *this*," she says, pointing to the sky and trees overhead.

And with that, I was nostril deep in a faith crisis—which, I don't mind saying, is embarrassing to admit.

It wasn't fair. I wasn't ready.

How was I to know that the company that gave us Mickey Mouse, Goofy, and *Son of Flubber* would venture deep into a religious debate? I was just minding my own business at thirty thousand feet over the Midwest and was caught off guard. Me—a professional Christian, a seminary professor paid to think right thoughts about God and to tell others about them. But after a long trip, my orthodoxy shield was resting at my side. I was unarmed, and Leslie's words hit their mark. In a flash and without words, I thought quietly to myself, *I think Leslie's right.*

The idea that the Creator of heaven and Earth, with all their beauty, wonder, and mystery, was at the same time a supersized Bible-thumping preacher, obsessed with whether our thoughts were all in place and ready to condemn us for eternity to hell if they weren't, *made no sense*—even though that was my operating (though unexamined) assumption as long as I could remember.

A fifty-two-second exchange in a movie—a *Disney movie,* for crying out loud (this is so embarrassing)—uttered by a fifth-grader and total outsider to the Christian faith. She doesn't even have a Ph.D. or fly across the country to academic conferences. And the next thing I know, my view of God flies away as if sucked out the window due to loss of cabin pressure.

Leslie's comment confronted me with a simple yet profound and uncomfortable question: When the dust clears and in the quiet of your own heart, what kind of God do you believe in, really? And why? I thought I had that all worked out. Yet, amazingly, with decades of church, Christian college, seminary, and graduate school behind me, and now a seminary professor, I had never actually asked myself that question to see what I thought. (And have I mentioned how embarrassing this is?)

But now I felt threatened, cornered into a moment of uncomfortably honest reflection. Leslie's comment was uttered with such effortless childlike commonsensical innocence, and it brought to the surface thoughts that had been safely tucked away for many years behind a thick wall of "proper Christian thinking." I had never openly explored my thinking about God because I was taught that questioning too much was not safe Christian conduct—it would make God *very* disappointed in me indeed, and quite angry.

So dangerous thoughts lay dormant, never entering my conscious mind. My theological antivirus software had been doing its job, working in the background to keep me from errors in thinking—until this stupid Disney movie snuck past and forced me to deal with it.

Jess's God was my default God, but Leslie's God was the one I, deep down, wanted to believe in. My inner May Belle reacted quickly—an aggressive panicked voice scolded me for slipping off the rails. After all, I wasn't calling into question some side issue of faith, like whether God wants me to give up chocolate or coffee for Lent, but a central question—perhaps *the* central question: What is God like?

Once you start down this path, there's no telling where the dominoes are going to fall—and then what? So I just sat there, trying not to think about it. But the train had pulled out of the station with me on it, and it was too late to jump off.

I didn't plan this little moment, and before I knew it my view of God passed from "Yeah, I got this" to "Uh-oh." Not triggered by an impressive book or lecture, the way it's supposed to for scholars. Not inspired while fasting or on a weekend prayer retreat, the way it's supposed to for the spiritually mature.

But a common and ordinary moment worked unexpectedly to snatch me from my safe, familiar, and unexamined spiritual neighborhood and plop me down somewhere I never thought I'd land. A forced spiritual relocation.

This episode and others like it resulted in a lot of spiritual wrestling matches, a change in employment, a change in churches, and even some breaks in relationships with other Christians. But while there has been much angst and some pain, there has also been a deepening, a maturation, a growth in my spirit that has led to closer intimacy with God.

I've come to accept these uh-oh moments rather than run from them. Precisely because they are unexpected, out of my control, and unsettling, they bear with them a lesson I need to hear: I need to be willing to let go of what I think I know, and trust God regardless. And I have come to trust that God uses these moments.

# Can We Just Be Honest for a Second, Please?

Most Christians—I'd be willing to bet, sooner or later, *all* Christians—have unexpected uh-oh moments that threaten familiar ways of believing and thinking about God, moments that show up without being invited, without a chance to prepare for what's coming and run for cover.

Maybe we've read a book, listened to a podcast, watched *Secrets of the Bible Revealed* on cable TV or a Disney movie on a plane that introduced instability to our once stable faith. Maybe we've met new people who don't share our ideas about the Bible or God at *all*, but who are just plain nice and what they say makes sense. Maybe we've experienced a deep loss or an unspeakable tragedy that leaves us questioning everything we ever thought we believed about God, the world, and our place in it.

I believe these uh-oh moments get our attention like nothing else can. In fact, I believe they are God moments. I don't claim to know how it all works, and I've learned the hard way over the years not to think I can speak for God, but I believe uh-oh moments serve a holy purpose—at least they have for me. They help break down the religious systems we create for ourselves that sooner or later block us from questioning, wondering, and, therefore, from *growing*.

For many of us, faith is our rock-solid source of security and hope. It provides the map and values for how we navigate the world. But life has all sorts of everyday and ordinary ways of upsetting our thinking about our faith. I believe that, in these moments, God invites us to deepen and grow in our relationship with and our understanding of God.

These are key moments of growth because we tend to create mental fortresses that keep us in the same safe religious space. It is upsetting to redraw our maps and change what we see as the anchor of our security—and if left to ourselves, we would never go there. So we build walls to prevent that from happening, walls within which we preserve what makes us feel secure, where we are in control and our God makes perfect sense to us.

Watching certainty slide into uncertainty is frightening. Our beliefs provide a familiar structure to our messy lives. They give answers to our big questions of existence: Does God exist? Is there a right religion? Why are we here? How do I handle suffering and tragedy? What happens to us when we die? What am I here for? Answering these questions provides our lives with meaning and coherence by reining in the chaos.

When familiar answers to those questions are suddenly carried away, like stray balloons at a county fair, we understandably want to chase after them to get them back. When once settled questions suddenly become unsettled, our life narratives are upset—and no one likes that.

Reflecting on that tension and working through it is what this book is about.

Another dynamic at work here is how friends, family, and church members would handle it if they knew what you were thinking. Feeling judged and banished is a common story among those who take a risk to let people in on their well-guarded secret.

Since I have outed myself as someone who is okay with questions about the faith, I can't tell you the number of private conversations I have had with people—often virtual strangers telling me about their secret questions and thoughts. They seem haggard and worried. Even frightened.

Taking a risk like this could mean being branded for life, that person who "used to have such strong faith" but is now just another doubter who "doesn't know what she believes anymore."

Church is too often the most risky place to be spiritually honest. What a shame. And when pastors and other Christian leaders are going through this, well, don't get me started. Those poor people. While they're working things through in private agony, they still have to keep up appearances or risk public shame, not to mention their paycheck.

So you hold it in and muddle through your life, keeping it all quiet, trying not to think about the lost faith you now mourn, and hoping nobody brings it up. Or, after you have tried to hold it in for a while, it may reach a point where the pressure is too much and explodes into a full-on crisis.

We need to talk about this.

Sooner or later we all find ourselves faced with some serious challenge to how we think about God. Don't we all eventually come to a crossroads where familiar beliefs don't work very well and we just don't really know what we believe anymore? Even if we have never verbalized it to ourselves (let alone to others), don't we all at some point have a nagging background noise of doubt, a deep undercurrent of cognitive dissonance, where what we were once so certain about evaporates like a dream?

# Okay, I'll Go First

I've certainly had some of those moments—and not just on air-planes. They're always uncomfortable and disorienting, and I just want them to go away. But I have come to trust—or at least I try to trust—that God is not calling me to resist these moments. I believe God patiently leads me through them.

I won't say my faith is "stronger"—that implies that the uh-ohs have been fixed or conquered, which is the opposite of what I am saying. I mean my faith is more real, more textured, three dimensional, and without the constant fear of being wrong playing in my head or that God is disappointed in me for not acing a multiple-choice theology exam.

One of my uh-oh moments happened when I left a spiritual community I had been a part of for twenty years. Leaving was challenging enough, but the really difficult moment ambushed me quietly and without warning several months later.

In my mid-twenties, I attended for four years a small conservative but sane seminary and then returned to teach there after earning my Ph.D. I would wind up spending another fourteen years there as a Bible professor, from my early thirties to mid-forties—about half my life at that point. That community deeply and powerfully shaped my thinking about the Bible, God, and life. That school was my spiritual home, more so than any church. It defined my faith. I couldn't imagine being anywhere else for the rest of my life.

I had some good years with fond memories. But toward the end of my time there, things began turning sour. We had a lot of quick turnover on the faculty, administration, and board—and that often leads to shifts in ideology. It was thought that things had become too relaxed, and now the school's conservative identity had to be protected. And with that, the atmosphere changed from collegial and generous to tense and adversarial. Our teaching and writing began to be closely monitored. It seemed like the slightest perceived deviations in thinking led to very serious meetings about the "future of the school" and "maintaining our heritage."

That was my experience.

The long and short of it is that I resigned after several stressful years. I will come back to that part of the story at the end of the book, because it is part of a larger story of how I began to trust God differently through all this. But for now, let me just say that I was ready to leave. Despite how much the school had meant to me spiritually, I was ready to leave. *Very* ready. So I did.

I recall those first few months of sweet freedom. I hadn't felt that light and joyful in probably a decade. Pick your cliché: I felt alive, born again, as if I had been liberated from a prison camp, released from a dungeon, and had seen the sunshine and felt the cool breeze for the first time in ages. And I had boundless energy. I was bursting at the seams with fresh and exciting ideas I felt free to put out there without threat of scolding. I wound up having seven books published within the next four years, which, frankly, is insane, but a lot of cramped thinking needed to stretch its legs. I even started eating well (fewer Oreos) and exercising for the first time in forever. I was taking care of myself emotionally and physically.

Life was great. But this newfound freedom and elation would also come with a cost, as I found out after about six months.

A fuse blew and faith went dark.

What happened?

My spiritual community with clearly defined boundaries and all sorts of intellectual no-go zones was suffocating, but it had one thing going for it: a spiritual territory was clearly marked out for me. I "knew" what I believed. I had some freedom to stroll about, of course, but guards were stationed at the towers to discourage me from venturing too close to the electric fence. Thinking for myself wasn't necessary and in fact was actively frowned upon. The heavy lifting was done for me. I just needed to agree and sign on the dotted line (literally—we signed a detailed statement of faith). That made for a safe, predictable life of faith.

In this model, *true faith* and *correct thinking* were two sides of the same coin—and that mentality had deeply formed my own spiritual identity. That's why faith went dark for me a few months after I left.

With no boundaries, nothing to sign, no Big Brother watching over my shoulder to make sure I maintained correct thinking, I was flying solo for the first time in half my life. It was up to me, not someone else, to forge a spiritual identity—just me and God with no one running interference.

And I wasn't ready for it.

A question began forming in my head, as if imposed by some outside force: *Well, Pete, you got what you wanted. No one's telling you what to think. So what* do *you think?*

Being confronted with that question was frightening—not frightening like *The Silence of the Lambs* or Trump 2016, but frightening like when you lose your bearings, when your life narrative looks more like a confused and jumbled mass of words on a page rather than the familiar story you knew and loved so well. Religious structure provides a sense of self. And now without it, I felt utterly alone, with no idea where all this was heading:

*What do you really believe, Pete, when no one is telling you what to believe? Who is God to you? Is there a God? How far are you willing to go to accept the challenge of this new journey where you can barely see your own hand in front of your face? What familiar road map are you willing to leave behind? What will you do now that God is no longer a turned back page in a familiar story you can flip to whenever? What will you do now that God is far off, out of sight? And how will you handle the likelihood that things will never be as they were?*

Seeking answers to those questions meant accepting the challenge of an unsettled faith. That takes courage, and if there is one part of my spiritual life that atrophied over the previous twenty years it was courage—the courage to think, to be honest, to be. I didn't know how to "do" faith without making sure my thoughts about God were lined up, and so, once those thoughts failed to be compelling, my faith sank.

For over a year, at home alone and out of work, I felt adrift at sea, treading water with no shoreline in sight, not knowing where the tide was taking me—and just as often not even caring.

My faith had transformed from "I know what I believe" to "I think I know." Then, as if bicycling down a steep hill with no brakes, it moved more quickly to

*I think I thought I knew,*

*I'm not so sure anymore,*
*I don't really know anymore,*
*Honestly, I have no idea,*
*Leave me alone.*

It felt like pressing factory reset so my software could reload. And as it did, I began to wonder, *Maybe . . . I need a major shift in my thinking.*

*Maybe knowing, as I had been taught to know, is overrated.*

*Knowing like that doesn't last.*

*Knowing has its place, definitely, but not at the center of faith.*

And then for me, the bottom line:

*I can choose to trust God with childlike trust regardless of how certain I might feel.*

I've come to see this process as sacred and ongoing. And it also takes courage—more courage and trust in God than I could have understood before.

# What's So Sinful About Certainty?

Our beliefs about God—which is to say our *thoughts* about God—are precious to us because they give us a sense of who we are and our place in this chaotic world. And we often can't imagine any other way of being "us." And so when our beliefs are threatened, the instinct, understandably, is to guard them fiercely, to resist any move as long as possible, to make the stress go away, and to stay in the comfort of our familiar spiritual homes.

But in resisting, we may actually be missing an invitation to take a sacred journey, where we let go of needing to be right and trust God regardless of what we feel we know or don't know.

The key to seeing this unsettling discomfort as a sacred rather than damning task is to decouple our *faith in* God from our *thoughts about* God. That way faith doesn't rest on correct thinking.

"What are you talking about, Enns?! My faith doesn't rest on my thoughts!"

Are you sure?

In ways we do not even perceive, we *all* create God in our own image. We may mean well and we may be motivated by our devotion toward God. But even when these ideas about God have proven very helpful to us, they become a hindrance to growth when the cement dries.

"Speak for yourself. I'm not creating God in my image. I'm just following the Bible."

No one just "follows" the Bible. We *interpret* it as people with a past and present, and in community with others, within certain traditions, none of which is absolute. Many factors influence how we "follow" the Bible. None of us rises above our place in the human drama and grasps God with pure clarity, without our own baggage coming along for the ride. We all bring our broken and limited selves into how we think of God.

We're human, in other words. We can't help but think of God in broken and limited ways, as creatures limited by time and space.

But that isn't the problem. In fact, the Christian faith declares that God freely and lovingly entered the human drama uniquely in one member of the human race, Jesus of Nazareth. God is okay with our humanity.

Here is the temptation: we can forget that we are human and delude ourselves into thinking that we can transcend our tiny place in the human drama and see from on high, as God sees. It turns out that is not really one of our options. *Walking the path of faith means trusting God enough to let our uh-oh moments expose how we create God to fit in our thinking.* But that is hard work. We like our ideas about God. We *need* them. And that is really the deeper problem here.

When we are held captive to our thinking, moving to what is not known and uncertain is automatically seen as a fearful development. We think true faith *is dependent* on maintaining a particular "knowledge set" and keeping a *firm grasp* on a tightly woven network of nonnegotiable beliefs, guarding each one vigilantly, making sure they all stay above the water line no matter how hard the struggle—because if what we "know" sinks, faith sinks right down with it.

Correct thinking provides a sense of certainty. Without it, we fear that faith is on life support at best, dead and buried at worst. And who wants a dead or dying faith? So this fear of losing a handle on certainty leads to a *preoccupation* with correct thinking, making sure familiar beliefs are defended and supported at all costs.

How strongly do we hold on to the old ways of thinking? Just recall those history courses where we read about Christians killing other Christians over all sorts of disagreements about doctrines few can even articulate today. Or perhaps just think of a skirmish you've had at church over a sermon, Sunday-school lesson, or which candidate to vote into public office.

*Preoccupation with correct thinking.* That's the deeper problem.

It reduces the life of faith to sentry duty, a 24/7 task of pacing the ramparts and scanning the horizon to fend off incorrect thinking, in ourselves and others, too engrossed to come inside the halls and enjoy the banquet. A faith like that is stressful and tedious to maintain. Moving toward different ways of thinking, even just trying it on for a while to see how it fits, is perceived as a compromise to faith, or as giving up on faith altogether. But nothing could be further from the truth.

Aligning faith in God and certainty about what we believe and needing to be right in order to maintain a healthy faith—these do not make for a healthy faith in God. In a nutshell, that is the problem. And that is what I mean by the "sin of certainty."

It is sin because this pattern of thinking sells God short by keeping the Creator captive to what we are able to comprehend—which is the very same problem the Israelites had when they were tempted to make images of God (aka idols) out of stone, metal, or wood. For ancient people, images made the gods present for the worshippers, something tangible to look at to let them connect with the divine realm. But Israel's God said no. Any images shaped by human hands limit God by bringing God too far into alignment with ancient conceptions of the divine.

We don't make physical images of God. But we do make mental ones.

I don't mean that our thoughts of God are no different than images of wood and stone. The images we read about in the Bible *always* limit God, because they confuse the Creator with creation. Thoughts about God, on the other hand, are not only often helpful but downright inevitable. When we confuse God with our thoughts about God, however, those thoughts *can* become idol-like—getting in the way of the real thing, hindering rather than aiding a life of faith.

When we grab hold of "correct" thinking for dear life, when we refuse to let go because we think that doing so means letting go of *God,* when we dig in our heels and stay firmly planted even when we sense that we need to let go and move on, *at that point we are trusting our thoughts rather than God.* We have turned away from God's invitation to trust in order to cling to an idol.

The need for certainty is sin because it works off of fear and limits God to our mental images. And God does not like being boxed in. By definition, God can't be. I believe we are prone to forget that. God is good to remind us—by any means necessary, if we are willing to listen. God understands our human predicament and is for us.

# Thinking Is Good

Let me be abso-posi-lutely clear about something so we don't get off on the wrong foot: there's absolutely nothing wrong with thinking about God or even seeking to think "correctly" about God.

Thinking about what we believe, learning more about what we believe, and disagreeing and deliberating with others, are normal for people of faith. At least I hope so, because I've just described pretty much the entire history of Christianity and Judaism, both of which are broad and deep when it comes to thinking and disagreeing about God. And as we'll see, debates and disagreements about God are in the Bible, too, because thoughts matter.

We humans are unimaginably complex psychological, physical, and spiritual beings. And thanks to a huge cerebral cortex, we are capable of something quite amazing: abstract thought, pondering the deep mysteries of life, ultimate meaning, and faith. The capacity to form thoughts about God, our place in the world, and how the two come together, is not only okay but an inevitable and sacred occupation given only to our species, a gift from God, I believe, that God invites us to use.

Personally, I can't help but think about the big questions of life and my own faith in particular. I went through nine years of seminary and doctoral work in biblical studies, not just to avoid getting a real job, but because I am naturally drawn to thinking about what I believe and why. I also like talking about what I think and tossing ideas back and forth, which is why I teach, blog, and write books like this one.

So I hope we are all on the same page here. I'm not saying that the life of the mind and working toward forming deeper thoughts about God are all bunk. The life of faith and the life of thought are not opposite ends of the spectrum.

Rather, I'm talking about a deeper, subtler, even subconscious problem that definitely isn't limited to Bible students or other sorts of eggheads but is part of the daily struggles of normal everyday Christians.

The deeper problem here is the *unspoken need* for our thinking about God to be right *in order* to have a joyful, freeing, healing, and meaningful faith.

The problem is trusting our beliefs rather than trusting God.

The preoccupation with holding on to correct thinking with a tightly closed fist is not a sign of strong faith. It hinders the life of faith, because we are simply acting on a deep unnamed human fear of losing the sense of familiarity and predictability that our thoughts about God give us. Believing that we are right about God helps give us a sense of order in an otherwise messy world. So when we are confronted with the possibility of being wrong, that kind of "faith" becomes all about finding ways to hold on with everything we've got to be right.

We are not actually trusting God at that moment. We are trusting ourselves and disguising it as trust in God.

Holding our thoughts with an open hand, however, is a way of communing with God—like an offering *to* God, incomplete as it may be.

This book is about thinking differently about faith, a faith that is not so much defined by *what* we believe but in *whom* we trust. In fact, in this book I argue that we have misunderstood faith as a *what* word rather than a *who* word—as primarily *beliefs about* rather than primarily as *trust in*.

Let me say again that beliefs themselves are not the problem. Working out what we believe is worthy of serious time and effort in our lives of faith. But our *pursuit* of having the right beliefs and locking them up in a vault are not the *center* of faith. Trust in God is. When holding to correct thinking becomes the center, we have shrunk faith in God to an intellectual exercise, a human enterprise, where differences need to be settled through debate *first* before faith can get off the ground.

A faith that *rests* on knowing, where you have to "know what you believe" *in order* to have faith, is disaster upon disaster waiting to happen. It values too highly our mental abilities. All it takes to ruin that kind of faith is a better argument. And there's always a better argument out there somewhere.

Christian faith is trusting in God, a personal being, rather than an abstract force. That's why we often refer to faith in God as having a "relationship" with God—which sounds like a Facebook status update, but it's true.

My beliefs or thoughts about a person are unavoidable, and often helpful in deepening the relationship—but they may not always be right, and the relationship shouldn't rest on getting them right. After all (and I know this may be hard to believe), I occasionally (by which

I mean often) have mistaken beliefs regarding my wife, which she is only too kind to point out to me. But this skewed knowledge does not nullify our marriage.

Our marriage is not based on accurate knowledge of each other we hold with confident certitude. Our vows are based on our commitment to trust and pursue one another, whether or not we understand each other correctly and regardless of whether the relationship is moving along swimmingly. Even if we don't like each other, annoy each other, or can't stand the sight of each other, the commitment to trust is fundamental. In fact trust is actually fundamental to being human. Children, as soon as they are conscious, trust their parents unconditionally and without deliberation. As we mature, trust is at the heart of any healthy relationship. Our relationship with God is no different.

Trust works regardless of where our thinking happens to be at the moment. But when correct thinking is central to faith, we transmit onto God our own distorted mental image of God, with all its baggage, hang-ups, and deep fears. That is a tense faith, which we cover up with cleverness and arrogance, and which slides easily to anger and hatred toward those who think differently.

When trusting God is central—even just the simple act of trying to trust when we might not feel like it—we are walking a holy path. When we learn that it is okay to let go of the *need* to be right—that God is not going to pounce on us from behind the corner and give us a whipping but actually welcomes this step of faith—only then will the debilitating stress of holding on to correct thinking begin to fade. Then we are giving control over to God, which is a more secure place for faith to rest than on the whims and moods of our own thinking.

The focus moves from ourselves to God, in whom we trust—what Jesus calls "dying" and "losing" our lives.

I believe this journey of learning to let go, of moving from the familiar to the unfamiliar, and thus learning truly to trust God is a journey of great courage and humility, and one I believe God wants us all to take, each of us in different ways, different times, different lengths, and for different reasons.

This journey is sacred and transforms us. And without that transformation, we will not be able to do the very thing both the Old Testament and New Testament* of the Christian Bible call our greatest religious obligations: to love God and neighbor (Deuteronomy 6:5; Leviticus 19:18; Luke 10:27).

That's what this book is about, and here is a bit more about where the book is headed.

First we'll look at how the preoccupation with correct thinking came to take such a hold on the Christian experience today (chapter 2). How did we get into this mess? Where did we make the wrong turn? And then we'll see what kind of faith the Bible models for us, a faith where we don't always feel certain but trust remains (chapters 3–5).

Watching how the biblical writers looked at faith as trust rather than certainty helps us through our inevitable uh-oh moments from a different perspective. These moments are not proof that faith

---

* I typically use the traditional designations of Old and New Testament to refer to the two parts of the Christian Bible. I warmly acknowledge that other Christian traditions, namely Roman Catholicism and Eastern Orthodoxy, include a few other books written in the centuries before Christ (aka the Apocrypha or deuterocanonical books), but I write as a Protestant (though a chastened one, I hope). Also, by referring to the writings of ancient Israel as "Old" Testament instead of Hebrew Bible, First Testament, or Tanach, I am not suggesting they are passé—as I think this book will illustrate again and again.

doesn't work, but only that a certain kind of faith doesn't work—one that needs correct thinking in order to survive (chapter 6).

We'll end by looking at how God's absence is God's way of addressing the sin of certainty (chapter 7), to cultivate in us a habit of trust that doesn't depend on certainty to survive (chapters 8–9).

A final note here: I do not want this book to be seen as merely for those who experience "problems of faith" or "crises of doubt" (though it is for those people). The problem is bigger. When we think of "strong" faith as something that *should* be free of uncertainty or crises, I believe we have gotten wrong an important part of who God is and how the Christian life really works. This book is about how we might address that problem.

Chapter
Two

# How We Got into This Mess

Happy are those who make the LORD their trust, who do not turn to the proud, to those who go astray after false gods.

—Psalm 40:4

# Know What You Believe (or Else)

Few if any truly come to faith in God by the sheer force of an argument. We come to faith for all sorts of reasons that aren't really "reasons" at all in the conventional sense. Our "reasons" are intuitive more than rational, emotional more than logical, mysterious more than known. I would say that coming to faith involves sensing God's presence, which may transcend or even defy our ability to rationally process the encounter.

This does not make faith less real or less stable. It simply acknowledges that faith is enmeshed in the fullness of our humanity and can never be reduced to an essentially intellectual process.

We do not come to faith lining up our thoughts and then venturing forth, and so why would it ever cross our minds that preoccupation with correct thinking is able—or necessary—to keep us there? Or why should anyone feel the need to depart from the path of faith—or be told they have to—because their experiences lead them to think differently than when they first came to faith?

The stumbling block here is our modern Western rational mindset, which has put on a golden throne the human capacity for rational thinking, our ability to know and explain our reality through our thoughts.

Don't misunderstand me. I value these God-given abilities and gifts we have. Humans are thinking creatures like no other. Also, I happen to like the modern world, what with its technology and all. Water and lights on demand, air travel, dental care, vaccines, anything battery powered. I'm not taking a cheap swipe at modernity, nor am I suggesting we turn the clock back to some bygone blissful era. We are who we are when we are. And it's all good.

But we also have to remember that we are more than walking brains, and truth isn't limited to what our minds can conquer. Christians, of all people, should know this, but too often they too seem to have bought into the modern project more than they might realize or want to admit.

Like a lot of Christians, I was taught—from a young age all the way through seminary, and in most every church I've ever been to, book I've read, or sermon I've heard—that having strong faith depends on "knowing what you believe." And people of true faith will be able to articulate what they know to a lost and blind world that just doesn't get it. It was all very logical and clear. Having that kind of sure knowledge of the mysteries of life is promoted as one of the major perks of being an insider to God.

Conversely, if you don't know what you believe, something is clearly wrong with you that needs to be addressed with a sense of some urgency. At least that is the message I picked up over the years—which really stinks if you happen to have questions and you don't always feel like you know what you believe.

I'm not trying to speak for all Christian traditions here. My tradition is Protestant, and I've experienced several versions of Protestantism on the broad evangelical spectrum. And there, "knowing what you believe" is a major, almost universal, preoccupation and cottage industry with defend-the-faith books, websites, seminars, and conferences.

For most of my life, going to church felt like another day of school, and that vibe seems to have been intentional. To get Sunday morning off on the right start, we were expected to attend an hour-plus, age-appropriate lesson called—in case it was unclear what was happening to you—Sunday school. And reading the right kinds of books on your own time was encouraged to learn more about what to believe and what not to believe.

Sermons were essentially the transmission of information and typically occupied center stage. They could easily last for half the service, often forty-five minutes or more, and consisted of "Bible expositions"—going from one verse to the next to explain what is there so you can know what is right and what is wrong to believe.

Other sermons might be on topics like marriage, evangelism, raising your teens, the upcoming election, or the Christian approach to watching the Super Bowl, but the vibe remained the same: the sermon is fundamentally a *lesson* that explained what the Bible (and therefore God) "says" about the matter at hand. And the sooner you know what the Bible/God says, the more confident you can be about your faith.

To help you retain that knowledge, taking notes on the sermon was encouraged or even expected. Church bulletins provided sermon outlines and empty space for that very purpose. Sermons were often taped and placed in a video/audio library for future reference, or in case you missed a Sunday and had to catch up.

Other parts of the service, like singing, praying, tithing, and communion (aka the Lord's Supper, or the Eucharist), were present and taken seriously, but they seemed like add-ons, intrusions to the main action, ramps to launch us up into the sermon and then down to the other side to provide closure. Information transmission was the hub around which the morning service turned. Sunday (and/or Wednesday) evening services would feature more talking and teaching. Missions work was supported, of course, but the expectation was that the church's distinctive knowledge set would be faithfully reproduced.

For most of my evangelical Christian life, the faith modeled for me was largely faith as an intellectual exercise, a series of information sessions, diagrams, handouts, and overheads so you could be certain about what you know you believe and go through life with unwavering confidence, ready and able to withstand attacks on your faith from your atheist college professors, Roman Catholics, CNN, or Oprah.

An upside is that personal Bible reading was expected. That can become another ball and chain, but I am also very thankful for this experience, for I got to know my Bible pretty well. Especially during trying times, passages I've absorbed through reading or hearing come to mind that help me remember that God and I have a past, and that past is still real in the present.

So I hope you don't hear me knocking the Bible or undermining learning about what you believe, in church or elsewhere. Not at all. Like I've been saying, knowing and learning about your faith is good and sacred. And neither am I throwing my former church tradition under the bus. God is there, too, and the people of God wind up in all sorts of traditions.

What I'm after here is how faith was taught and modeled—as a preoccupation with correct thinking, which feeds on the mentality that *knowing* (especially the Bible) is *central* to faith. That message was clear as a bell. Knowing what you believe places faith on solid, unshifting ground. At least that was the plan.

That idea began to crumble for me rather quickly, in my thirties and especially my forties—a bit of which I talked about last chapter. Life got messy. By "life" I mean a wife, three children, a career, and financial responsibilities; illness, stress, crisis, pain, death. You know, life. My experience kept being out of sync with what I "knew" about God, the world, and what it means to live in it. Familiar ways of thinking yielded less and less certainty. My life of spiritual training, where needing to know was dominant, had set me up perfectly for trouble.

I'm guessing I'm not alone here. If you can't relate at all, you might be a toddler (and major props just for reading this far), or you started your journey of faith sometime in the last six hours.

As life got messier and more complicated, I came to see—here and there, now and then, or at times with sudden, crashing clarity—how much my entire existence was actually out of my control, and in fact always had been. But I never paid enough attention to dig deeper. I had always been too busy assuming my thought world was up for the task. But life won, as it always does, which rocks us off our knowledge perch. Yet "know what you believe" was the center of my spiritual training and support for most of my life. My faith was no help. It was actually part of the problem.

Looking back, I am simply astounded that *no one was aware enough to tell any of us that sooner or later "know what you believe" wouldn't cut it.* Sooner or later, that tank runs empty.

I don't judge myself too harshly, at least in my better moments, for not grasping this rather obvious point sooner. I was young and caught up in it all. But still, surely someone older and wiser had to have known all this, right? Or perhaps in a knowledge-based faith no one felt safe saying it—like a corporate CEO saying, "You know folks, money isn't central to what we do here."

Neither do I hold anyone else responsible for my experience. For one thing, at the end of the day, we are all responsible for what we do. No one blackmailed me or held me hostage. And playing the blame game only keeps us looking in the rearview mirror, which is a sure recipe for misery.

But another reason I don't blame any church is that conservative Western churches as a whole are simply caught up in something bigger and older than themselves. Knowledge-based faith, and hence a preoccupation with correct thinking in order to have faith, is a deep, systemic, and largely unquestioned condition of much of Western Christian culture—like construction detours, bank holidays, and free birthday breakfasts at Denny's. It is what it is.

I was caught in a conflict that had been festering for centuries.

# Oh Great, We Came from Monkeys

Depending on where you live, you might see churches dotting the landscape, with names like Crossroads Bible Church, Main Street Bible Church, Bible Baptist Church, and so on. In my neck of the woods, hardly the Bible Belt but still with a long Christian heritage, a Google search shows me about a dozen "Bible" churches within a half-hour ride.

These churches, along with Bible seminaries and Bible colleges, are monuments to a rocky time in the not too distant past that has left its stamp all over contemporary conservative Christian America—the so-called Fundamentalist-Modernist Controversy of the late nineteenth and early twentieth centuries. Think Scopes Monkey Trial.

*Hey!!! Wake up! Pay attention! This isn't a boring history lesson. It's why our churches do what they do.*

Here's what happened. Intellectually speaking, the Protestant Christian faith in America had been doing pretty well for itself for a long time. Christianity was considered "reasonable," even common-sensical, and Christian leaders and laypeople generally assumed that the Bible was a book of accurate history and science, and defending it was as easy as pointing to a verse to prove your point. And there was no reason to think otherwise. That is, until the nineteenth century got in the way.

The idea of the Bible providing a sure intellectual foundation for what we believe took a knockout blow from four rapid punches to the chin within about thirty years. The first punch is also the best known: Charles Darwin and the theory of evolution.

The idea didn't actually start with Chuck, but he gets the credit for putting the big picture together and getting the word out (in his famous book *On the Origin of Species*).* As the story goes, sometime after he was bird watching on the Galapagos Islands, Darwin came to see that all the diverse life-forms on Earth are connected through "common descent" and evolved through a process of "natural selection." But what most people heard was, "We came from monkeys."

The problem for biblically centered Christians is that the Bible, right in the very beginning, tells us clearly that God created all life-forms with a simple "Let there be . . ." No common descent, natural selection, or billions of years required. So if Darwin was right, the Bible was wrong—and most of the scientific and academic world thought Darwin, scientifically speaking, nailed it. Darwin's theory was bound to get some push back, and the Scopes Monkey Trial of 1925 was the public cage match between modernity (science) and fundamentalism (the Bible is right no matter what science says).

The controversy over evolution never quite went away, and in

---

* This is as good a time as any to tell you that I've included notes at the end of the book that give a bit more information on a few things, the sources I used, and/or some reading suggestions. Take a peek. The notes are listed in order, with the chapter and section clearly indicated, along with a few words to prompt what I am commenting on. I'm doing everything I can to avoid disrupting the flow of the book by inserting those annoying endnote numbers. If you're so inclined, it might be easiest to scan the notes first as you begin reading each chapter so you can see what's coming.

fact has gone through a revival of sorts in recent years. "New Atheists" like Richard Dawkins (*The God Delusion*) practically trip over themselves for the joy of sticking evolution in the face of Christian fundamentalists and evangelicals in books, TV, and social media.

And it doesn't help that scientists have recently mapped the human genome. Don't ask me to explain that, but based on books I've read and conversations I've had, the genomes of humans and primates are so strikingly similar that they have to be related to each other. That means, genetically speaking, we can't speak of a "first couple"—Adam and Eve—as the Bible says. The study of genetics seems to be a slam-dunk-over-the-defense-break-the-backboard proof for evolution—a first couple is genetically impossible. And the fact that an evangelical Christian, Francis Collins, led an international team responsible for mapping the human genome has made it an even harder pill for some to swallow.

Throw into the mix what geologists have known since at least the eighteenth century from the fossil record and rock sedimentation: the earth isn't a few thousand years old, as the writers of the Bible likely assumed, but several billion years old—4.5 billion, to be exact.

And since we're getting all this science stuff out of our system, astrophysicists in recent generations have described for us a universe that is so large and so old I don't even want to talk about it—other than to say the "known universe" is about 13.8 billion years old, and it would take something like 93 billion years to get from one end to the other traveling at the speed of light. Let me go on record and say this is beyond our comprehension, and Genesis looks like a children's story by comparison.

Science in general and evolution in particular made knowledge-based Christians in the nineteenth century with Bibles in hand very nervous, and for good reason. And things haven't gotten much better.

# Seriously Weird Stories
# from Long Ago

Around the same time that Darwin published his research, Christians got a second punch in the jaw.

For most of Christian history, our source of information about the ancient Israelites and their neighbors was the Bible alone. Other ancient peoples hardly had an independent voice.

That began to change in the nineteenth century when some curious archaeologists began digging in the Middle East to uncover the ancient past. (I have a rather hefty but scintillating note on this at the end of the book.) Beforehand, digging was largely up to amateurs and grave robbers selling ancient artifacts on the black market. Professional archaeologists introduced some respect for the ancient world. They used careful methods for digging and recording what was found—like bones, houses, temples, weapons, monuments, and tablets with writing on them.

These efforts have helped us put the biblical story of the Israelites in a wider context. Now we have a chance to let some of these other nations speak for themselves, to see what they thought, what they believed. And some of what archaeologists discovered has led to major turning points in how we see the Bible and the ancient Israelites. And in the early years of archaeology, the victim, once again, was the book of Genesis.

It turns out that other ancient nations had their own stories of beginnings, and they were similar to the stories in Genesis—creation, the first humans, and a great flood that drowned everyone. These other stories were not only *similar* but also much *older* than the versions we find in the Bible. So, logically speaking, if the biblical versions of these stories are *similar* and *younger,* the biblical writers likely weren't working from scratch. They had a formula for writing their stories.

The idea that the stories in Genesis were later versions of older ones made a lot of Christians uncomfortable. The Bible didn't look unique any longer, a book with classified information from God delivered only to the ancient Israelites. It looked more like another story told by a tribal people from three thousand or so years ago, with a talking serpent and two trees with "magical" properties to give life and knowledge. These stories were myths—stories of deep religious value written by and for ancient people with no (or precious little) historical, let alone scientific, value for us today.

So now Christians in the nineteenth century had to deal with evolution and archaeology. Many would find it difficult to go on as if nothing had happened. It looked more and more like the book of Genesis was wrong about science and history.

All this contributed a very serious period of freaking out and set Bible-believing Christians on a long course of being preoccupied with correct thinking, namely "defending the faith" by defending the Bible as scientifically and historically accurate—if not in every detail, then at least "basically" accurate. Certainly not myths adopted from pagan neighbors. After all—as the logic goes—if the Bible couldn't be relied upon to provide certainty about how the world began and where people come from, it couldn't really be trusted for much else. Therefore the viability of the Christian faith—based on the Bible—was in peril.

And there's more. (Are we having fun yet? No? Neither were nineteenth-century Christians.)

# The Germans Are Coming
# (Like We Need This Right Now)

As if landing two hard punches against the ropes wasn't enough, a third blow came from Germany—specifically from German biblical scholars who had been doing their scholarship thing for over two hundred years already. And once again, the victim was poor old battered Genesis, though now the next four books of the Bible were also affected. (The first five books—Genesis, Exodus, Leviticus, Numbers, and Deuteronomy—together make up the Pentateuch, "five scrolls," aka the Law of Moses, or the Torah.)

Here's what happened. Since forever it was thought that Moses, after leading the Israelites out of Egypt, wrote down in his old age all or most of the first five books of the Bible in the fifteenth century BCE. But careful readers of the Pentateuch—long before the nineteenth century—had seen problems with this scenario. The Pentateuch has some obvious logical inconsistencies, contradictions, stories told from different perspectives, and bears the marks of different writing styles and, in some cases, of a much later time. (I unpack this a bit in the note at the end of the book.)

Biblical scholars across the board came to the same conclusion. It seemed to them that several people, living centuries apart and long after Moses, wrote various portions of these books, which were then edited together about one thousand years after Moses lived. Similar to Darwin's theory of evolution, this theory of the "evolution" of the Pentateuch was almost universally convincing to scholars at the time. And that caused a crisis.

If God's appointed messenger Moses wrote the Pentateuch, then you would have a God-appointed eyewitness to at least four of the five books. Moses arrives on the scene in the second book (Exodus) and dies in the fifth book (Deuteronomy). Four out of five books with Moses around ain't bad. So, as the logic goes, if the bulk of Pentateuch was written by the eyewitness Moses, we can be reasonably sure that the Pentateuch is *historically accurate*. But if biblical scholars were correct and the Pentateuch had several authors and then one editor one thousand years after Moses's time, you've got a major blow to the Bible being an accurate account of history—which is the same problem introduced by evolution and archaeology.

So we have Darwin, archaeology, and now the Germans—three hard punches landing square on the jaw of the Bible all within about a thirty-year period of the nineteenth century, and the Bible was down for the count. The first five books of the Bible don't give us accurate science or history recorded by an eyewitness. Rather, the Pentateuch that we have in our Bibles is as far removed from the time of Moses as we today are removed from the Norman conquest of England (1066 CE, so you don't have to look it up like I did).

And this theory wasn't staying put in the secluded halls of academia. It was spreading to churches of Europe and America. Conservatives were deeply worried—*panicked* is the right word—that this would cause average churchgoers to lose their *faith* because it challenged their *thinking* about the Bible. I feel their pain. Their panic was justified—but only because faith and correct thinking were seen as two sides of the same coin.

Conservative Protestant churches have never fully recovered from these blows. In American evangelical and fundamentalist Christian colleges and seminaries today, the "battle for the Bible" begun in the nineteenth century continues to rage against these three "attacks" on the Bible. Indeed, the battle must be waged. The Christian faith itself is at stake.

But a fourth blow was yet to come—in some respects more devastating than the other three.

# Slavery: Whose Side Is God On?

Christians in the nineteenth century debated whether kidnapping, buying and selling, and enslaving Africans was all part of God's plan. Both sides looked to the Bible for sure moral guidance for solving this conflict. And both sides found what they needed, not so much because they were biased readers (although they were), but because the Bible itself gives conflicting information about slavery.

On the one hand, slavery in the Bible was a given, and slaves were the property of the owner, just as in every other ancient society. The Bible even contains laws about how to treat slaves that should make us squirm.

> When a slaveowner strikes a male or female slave with a rod and the slave dies immediately, the owner shall be punished. But if the slave survives a day or two, there is no punishment; for the slave is the owner's property. (Exodus 21:20–21)

I wonder whether African slaves ever felt like God had painted a number on their backs.

A favorite go-to Bible verse for slave owners was the story of the flood where Noah curses one of his grandsons, Canaan, to be the "lowest of slaves" (Genesis 9:25). It just so happened that, according to the flood story, the descendants of Canaan were among those who migrated to the African continent. I imagine slaveholders were quite happy to read right in the Bible that their slaves were descendants of the accursed first slave Canaan. And passages like this from the New Testament certainly helped their case:

> Slaves, obey your earthly masters with fear and trembling, in singleness of heart, as you obey Christ; not only while being watched, and in order to please them, but as slaves of Christ, doing the will of God from the heart. (Ephesians 6:5–6; see also Colossians 3:22 and Titus 2:9)

Slaveholders were like Jesus, demanding and deserving obedience from their subjects.

On the other hand, some saw the exodus story as proof that God is in the business of liberating slaves. The Bible also has a rather wonderful provision for releasing slaves after six years and for harboring escaped slaves who wind up on your doorstep (Exodus 21:2 and Deuteronomy 23:15). We also read that masters must treat their slaves "justly and fairly," which is at least a start in the direction of humanizing slaves (Colossians 4:1 and Ephesians 6:9). And at one point, Paul just comes out and says this:

> There is no longer Jew or Greek, there is no longer slave or free, there is no longer male and female; for all of you are one in Christ Jesus. (Galatians 3:28)

We could go on, but the point is that the Bible gives conflicting moral guidance, which caused for everyday people a different kind of crisis of faith than the one caused by Darwin, archaeology, and some Germans. It's one thing for the Bible to be wrong about the long-ago past (as difficult as that was to process), but it is far worse for the Bible to be of no use to us here and now when we actually need it to tell us what to do.

If you can't trust the Bible to tell you what to do on such a pressing moral issue of the day, than what is it good for? In what sense is the Bible God's word when it looks like we can't count on it to steer us through the real and urgent complexities of life? And so the Bible didn't seem trustworthy—either for telling us about the past or for navigating the present.

With all of this, the dominoes were unwinding down the slippery slope (that's a clever mixed metaphor—think about it), and the only way to hold it all together, the only way to hold tight to "what we know," was to hunker down and defend the Bible. As the Bible goes, so does Christianity.

This is why we see such a preoccupation with the transmission and preservation of knowledge among evangelical and fundamentalist churches in America today —the reason they "do church" the way they do. They have been living in intellectual reactive mode for generations to defend the intellectual certainty that they believe the Bible needs to provide. That is why Bible churches and colleges began popping up around the turn of the twentieth century and continue to thrive. That is why such a premium is placed on Sunday school, long lecture-like sermons, and reading the right books and keeping away from bad ones.

Of course, not every contemporary pastor or leader is aware of this history, but it's still in their DNA, passed on from one generation to the next. Patrolling their borders is part of the job description. The faith is at stake, and the skirmishes have been known to get pretty nasty. If having faith means holding on to certainty, when certainty is under "attack," your only option as a good Christian is to go to war—even if that means killing your own.

# Again with the Germans

So are you bored yet? I hope not. I can't really help you with that anyway, plus you're just going to have to be bored for another couple of pages, because we're going to talk about Martin Luther in order to get the bigger picture of how we got into this mess.

Martin Luther (died 1546) was a German monk. He also reportedly drank a lot of beer. Whether that's relevant or not, Luther had issues with the Roman Catholic Church. The long and short of it was that the Church was obscuring what he felt the gospel was all about—God's forgiveness of our sins by God's absolutely free mercy and love. One does not earn God's forgiveness.

One thing that set Luther off was that the Church had gotten into the indulgences market, which was very much about earning forgiveness. An indulgence, to put it a bit crassly, was a way of donating money for a new church building in return for having your sins forgiven, along with the sins of those who have already died and are presently stuck in purgatory (a place of purification after death to make you ready to enter heaven eventually). Perhaps not medieval Catholicism's finest hour.

Luther wasn't the first to say "Uh . . . excuse me, but NO" to indulgences, but he parlayed his *protests* to the point where he called for sweeping *reforms* of the Church—which is why it's called the Protestant Reformation. And here is why this is important for us: Luther's rallying cry was that the Bible alone (*sola scriptura,* to use the Latin phrase) was to be the basis of these reforms, because the Bible alone—not decrees handed down by a fallible Church hierarchy—has the imprint of God's authority on it.

Luther did not succeed in reforming the Catholic Church, so he started another one, eventually called the Lutheran church, which claimed to follow the teachings of the Bible more carefully. But in doing so, one problem was solved and many others were created—and with that, we are getting even closer to my point.

If the Bible alone is seen as the final court of appeal for right thinking about God and how one lives a life of faith, it becomes vitally important that you *get the Bible right* and that everyone is on the same page about what "right" means. And to help ensure that everyone had access to the Bible to do just that, Luther translated the whole Bible from the original Hebrew (Old Testament) and Greek (New Testament) into German, thus putting the Bible into the hands of every "Joe Meatball and Sally Housecoat."*

And once you translate the Bible into a language people actually speak and understand, they are bound to start forming opinions about what the Bible "says."

Anyone who has ever been to a church Bible study or—heaven help us—led one, knows what's coming next. When people read the Bible for themselves, they often disagree about what it means. The

---

* C. Montgomery Burns, referring to the commoners of Springfield, on *The Simpsons.*

Bible does not have a good track record of promoting unity among those who read it. Take us back to the carefree days of the papacy and the few who interpreted the Bible for the many. At least you had some order. Now you have chaos.

In time, Protestant denominations were popping up like dandelions—Baptists, Anabaptists (Mennonites), Calvinists, Methodists, and on and on. They all agreed that getting the Bible right was the first priority, because getting the Bible right was the key to getting the Christian faith right. The problem, though, was that they each thought they carried that key in their pocket and kept it safe for the rest. And this is why Protestant church softball games even to this day sometimes end in a brawl. (I was actually in one once.)

And here's something else about Luther and the Protestant Reformation: Luther's Germany, and elsewhere in Europe, is also where modern biblical scholarship would take root within two hundred years.

Feel free to draw a line from one to the other. Luther championed independence from Church tradition so he could follow where the Bible led. It wasn't long before some—who read and thought a lot, too, but were also largely fed up with the whole church thing in general—said, "How about independence from *any* church tradition and seeing where *that* takes us?"

Soon you had university professors reading the Bible without feeling they needed to line up with *any* church doctrine. They took the Protestant you're-not-the-boss-of-me spirit to the next level. *Sola scriptura* for the Reformers never meant ignoring church tradition. But now *sola scriptura* went into hyperdrive: the Bible alone *without any outside church authority* to tell us what is says. The only authority was "the natural light of reason."

The end result of all this upheaval in Germany beginning in the seventeenth century, and soon elsewhere in Europe, was that the Bible wasn't a perfect holy book from God, but a book from long ago and far away, and had to be studied by scholars like any other ancient text. The gates were flung open to read the Bible apart from and even against church tradition, Catholic or Protestant.

And with that, the modern period of biblical studies was born, which continued to grow and mature until it hit its major growth spurt into full adulthood, as we've seen, in the nineteenth century.

# Why "Defenders of the Faith" Are Raising White Flags

If you've made it this far, relax. It's over. No more history. And at least you can say you accomplished something today.

For the record, I don't think grappling with what the Bible says is a bad move. But when we take a step back from how church happens today for many of us, we can see that we are part of a legacy where getting the Bible "right" is important, even central. So on one level, we can't rightly hold any church or movement today fully responsible for being preoccupied with correct thinking and making sure their beliefs are rock solid and certain. It goes with the territory.

But this long history has begun taking a surprising turn in recent decades—and that brings us to why I wanted to write this book in the first place. After a few hundred years of various groups claiming to have a firm handle on getting the Bible right, a critical mass of Protestants is starting to wonder whether this quest for certainty is running on fumes.

If we are supposed to know what we believe and be sure of it, and if that knowledge comes to us from the Bible, how come there are thousands (literally) of Protestant churches out there, each claiming to be biblical? What's wrong with this picture? Are we to think that one of them is basically right and the others basically wrong? Or that perhaps this mess is an indication that we may have been walking down the wrong road?

And that's the great irony here. The long Protestant quest to get the Bible right has not led to greater and greater certainty about what the Bible means. Quite the contrary. It has led to a staggering number of different denominations and subdenominations that disagree sharply about how significant portions of the Bible should be understood. I mean, if the Bible is our source of sure knowledge about God, how do we explain all this diversity? Isn't the Bible supposed to *unify* us rather than divide us?

In a sense, the fact that churches continue being preoccupied with correct thinking is perfectly understandable: holding to what you know is part of the Protestant DNA, passed down to contemporary evangelicalism and fundamentalism via the Fundamentalist-Modernist Controversy. But that preoccupation is also inexcusable, because we only need to google "churches in my area" to see that this road of getting the Bible right has led, if not to a complete dead end, then at least to an endless traffic circle.

This struggle between fundamentalists and modernists over the Bible has also revealed an odd fact lying just below the surface. Even though these two groups see the Bible in polar opposite ways, they share the *same starting point:* any book worthy of being called God's word would need to talk about the past accurately. The modernists, looking at things like the problems with Genesis, concluded that the Bible wasn't, after all, a supernatural book that told us reliable facts about the past.

Fundamentalists fought back. They said the modernists showed lack of faith in God by doubting that the Bible gives an accurate record of history. The Bible, *because* it is God's word, *must* get the past right. Otherwise the whole Christian faith collapses. This attitude spawned a long history of fundamentalist crusades to defend the Bible against modernist "attacks" by amassing their own arguments for why the Bible can be fully trusted as a historical document despite what mainstream academics say.

These crusades are still very much part of Christian culture, at least in America. But the question many are asking today, as I am in this book, is whether the Bible is really set up in the first place to give the kind of certainty that both of these groups expected. Is the Bible's role really to give us certainty about what happened in the past (and to be judged thumbs up or down)? Perhaps the endless back-and-forth debates were rooted in the wrong question.

I believe that the Bible does not model a faith that depends on certainty for the simple fact that the Bible does not provide that kind of certainty. Rather, in all its messy diversity, the Bible models trust in God that does not rest on whether we are able to be clear and certain about what to believe.

In fact, the words "belief" and "faith" in the Bible are just different ways of saying "trust." And trust works, regardless of where our knowing happens to be.

# "You Abandoned Me, God; You Lied" (and Other Bible Lessons)

Listen to the sound of my cry, my King and my God,
for I cry to you.

—Psalm 5:2

# Parts of the Bible We Don't Read in Church (but Should)

This may be hard to hear, and you might want to be sitting down, but as my children got into their teens, especially my daughters, they did not worship the ground I walked on. They actually found flaws in me, their father.

During one particularly rough patch, I asked my youngest daughter, Sophie, who was around sixteen at the time, why she seemed to be avoiding me, had hardly acknowledged me for weeks, and (can you believe this?) refused my friend request on Facebook. She looked me square in the eye and said in a matter-of-fact, logical tone of voice, "Because I don't like you." Well, that did it. I'm a failure. I fell into self-pity mode with a healthy dash of passive-aggressive behavior toward Sophie.

Somewhere in my brooding, I mentioned this to a more seasoned parent, who had a good chuckle over it.

"Good for you!" he said.

"Excuse me?"

"For Sophie to say this—free of screaming and drama—means that she trusts you enough to be honest with you. You've got a healthy dynamic going on here. Trust is deep, unquestioned, sort of a reflex. Good parenting job!"

From failure to Father of the Year. Not bad.

Which brings me to the book of Psalms in the Old Testament—those 150 poems of faith that ancient Israelites sung or read in worship to God.

Walk into the Bible section of bookstores and you'll find, alongside the normal unabridged version of the Bible, stand-alone copies of the New Testament with the book of Psalms tucked inside. It's not hard to guess why—"The Lord is my shepherd," "Yea, though I walk through the valley of the shadow of death." Things like that.

The Psalms have a reputation for being uplifting, that practical part of the Old Testament that's actually useful, leaving all those begats, laws, and endless stories of Israel's kings for those with more time on their hands. Publishers know what Christians want to hear. Plus, the Psalms *are* great. Christians and Jews have gained much solace and encouragement from them over the centuries.

But they aren't all "Praise the Lord." Some psalms are desperate and bracingly honest cries for help in the face of trouble and danger. And a few—the ones I want to talk about—are downright startling, even unsettling, in how they talk about God. We never seem to get around to reading those parts in church, but they have *a lot* to tell us about the life of faith—and why a preoccupation with correct thinking is off topic.

The unsettling psalms, those that aren't on their best Sunday behavior, have a lot to say about trusting God precisely *because* they go to those dark places of faith. These psalms deserve to be read a lot, not ignored or tamed to shield us from the pain of the faith crises we read about there.

They might actually become close friends over time, the kind that just listen to you vent without judging you.

The 150 Psalms we have in our Bible are basically of three types:

1. Everything is fine. God is great. Stay the course.
2. Things are terribly wrong, and I am at the end of my rope, but thank you Lord for coming to my rescue (alternate ending: I know you'll come to my rescue soon/eventually).
3. Things are terribly wrong, I am at the end of my rope, and to make things worse, Oh Lord, you're nowhere to be found.

The first two types of psalms are more common than the third, but those deep laments are still there in the Bible, staring at us, daring us to read them word for word. And these psalms don't flinch.

A barrier has arisen between these writers and God—and they get right in God's face and hold God fully responsible, like a forgotten child waiting hours after school to be picked up by a distracted parent. They don't hesitate to question God's trustworthiness. Some wonder whether God is worth their time.

One of my favorite in-your-face psalms is Psalm 88. Let me summarize:

O Lord, I have been on my knees to you night after night. I am so troubled, and in so much agony, I feel like I have one foot in the grave, in deep and dark places. I am absolutely without hope, including in you. You really don't seem to care.

Actually, let me be blunt: you've abandoned me and so this is all your fault. You're the one who makes me feel like this.

You're even the one responsible for my own friends looking at me like I'm some sort of freak show.

Even so, all night and all day I'm on my knees praying, still calling to you for some relief—I'm desperate. But you keep on hiding. I'm in absolute pain and the only friend I have is darkness. Thanks for nothing.

Feel free to call this a faith crisis.

It's hard to imagine talking like this in church. Letting your guard down and bearing your soul with this degree of raw honesty is risky. You might find yourself in the middle of a protect-you-from-atheism intervention prayer phone chain faster than you can say "Bill Maher." Or you might be judged as a weak or uncommitted Christian and shunned.

What's this psalmist's problem? Doesn't he know he needs to be a rock-solid Israelite, a model of confidence for others, a super saint? At least doesn't he know not to put problems in writing for everyone to see?

Maybe this guy just doesn't know his Bible well enough. Or maybe he needs to go to another Bible study or listen to some sermon tapes so he can learn he shouldn't feel this way. What weak faith. Let's keep him away from our children. In fact, let's ask him to stay home until this unfortunate season of weak faith blows over, lest his negative attitude affect the rest of us happy and truly faithful people.

Ugh.

Ever wonder why the ancient Israelites not only wrote things like this but *kept them . . . forever . . . in their sacred book*?

Are they preserved as examples of what *not* to think or say, perpetual reminders of how *not* to feel and think, cones and red flares along the smoothly paved highway of faith warning us of "danger ahead"?

Nah.

Feeling like God is far away, disinterested, or dead to you is part of our Bible and can't be brushed aside. And that feeling—no matter how intense it may be, and even offensive as it may seem—is never judged, shamed, or criticized by God. Worshipping other gods or acting unjustly toward others gets criticized about every three sentences, but not this honest talk of feeling abandoned by God.

And let's not forget, the Gospels tell us that Jesus himself experienced God's abandonment on the cross, and he uses a ready and waiting psalm to express his feelings: "My God, my God, why have you forsaken me?" (Psalm 22:1; Matthew 27:46; Mark 15:34). We're in good company.

These expressions of abandonment aren't godless moments, evidence that something is wrong and needing to be fixed. They relay the experiences of ancient men and women of *faith,* and were kept because those experiences were common—*part of being an Israelite and therefore valued.* For us they signal not only what *can* happen in the life of faith, but also what *does* happen—what we should *expect* to happen.

I'm glad Psalm 88 doesn't end on a good note. It just leaves you there: "You have caused friend and neighbor to shun me; my companions are . . . darkness" (verse 18).* Don't we all, at one point or another, feel our lives are a deep pit of blah, where we are completely alone, our best friends are grief and depression—and God is the reason why?

---

* The NRSV has "my companions are *in* darkness," but "in" isn't in the Hebrew and the sense is more unsettling, as it should be, without it.

Old Testament theologian Walter Brueggemann calls these parts of the Bible Israel's "countertestimony." They challenge the "main testimony," those parts of the Bible where things are moving along more or less as scripted. We need this countertestimony, as did the Israelites, because no one lives in the scripted places of the Bible all the time, where God shows up as planned, tells us exactly what we need to do, and things work out.

Most of us probably live much of our lives in Psalm 88—in that place where our spiritual scaffolding has crumbled, and we are no longer so sure about God or much else. What we thought we knew, what we could be certain of and count on, turns out not to be certain at all. And we are left shaking our fist at God.

I feel that my spiritual leaders were motivated to shield me from those feelings, or look down on me for having them. I was never told to embrace the fact that faith looks like this sometimes. What a shame. People like me, and I imagine most of us, need to hear we are not alone. That's why this psalm is my favorite, and I'm glad it's in the Bible.

# God Is a Liar

Wait, did I say Psalm 88 was my favorite? I'm sorry. I meant to say Psalm 89, the one where the writer sets up God as totally awesome and then calls God a liar.

Here's how the psalm begins:

> I will sing of your *steadfast love*, O LORD, *forever;*
>> with my mouth I will proclaim your *faithfulness*
>> to all generations.
> I declare that your *steadfast love* is established *forever;*
>> your *faithfulness* is as *firm as the heavens.*
> (89:1–2; emphasis added)

Apparently, God is all about steadfast love and faithfulness toward Israel—which isn't simply a description of God's *feelings* but of God's *actions,* which are unwavering, unfaltering, as "firm as the heavens"* themselves. This psalmist seems to be on top of the world, beside himself with praising God.

---

* We read in Genesis 1:6–8 that God fashioned a solid dome overhead that stretched from horizon to horizon, enclosing a flat Earth. Picture a snow globe with a flat bottom.

What's he so happy about, exactly? He takes the next thirty-five verses to lay it out, and it's all about a solemn promise God had made to Israel hundreds of years earlier: an unbreakable promise ("covenant") to King David (2 Samuel 7:1–17). David's reign would be glorious, and then, beginning with David's son Solomon, God's *steadfast love* would stay with David's descendants "forever" (which in the Old Testament means not literally "never ending" but "so long into the future you don't have to worry your little heads about it").

On top of that, as the psalmist goes on to tell us, this promise-making God also happens to be the Creator of the cosmos, the ruler of the earth, sea, and sky. None of the gods of the other nations can compare, and so with the Almighty Creator on Israel's side making a solemn promise to David and his descendants, they can't lose. Good times.

The psalmist goes on like this, praising God for being the Creator, pausing now and then to remind everyone that this God, the Creator and ruler of the cosmos, is *steadfast* and *faithful*. God would see to it that David and his line would endure *as long as the heavens endure*—which seems rather permanent, for all practical purposes. The king and his people will never be without God's protection, striking down their foes like flies. You can count on God. All those who worship this God are happy and secure.

In fact, this promise places no obligation on any of David's descendants to hold up their end of the bargain. Even if any were to disobey God's laws and God would need to punish them, the promise remains guaranteed: "I will not remove from him my *steadfast love*, or be false to my *faithfulness*. I will not violate my covenant, or alter the word that went forth from my lips" (Psalm 89:33–34).

The vibe I'm picking up—and that the psalmist wants us to pick up—is that the Almighty Creator made a promise with no expiration date. This God *cannot* renege on that promise because he is steadfast, and this God *is able* to remain true to the promise because this God is the Creator. If this God were to renege, he would be breaking the promise, and that would make God a liar—which is impossible, because if there's anyone you can count on to keep his promises, it's the steadfast, loving, Almighty Creator God.

Unless you're reading Psalm 89.

Here's the problem. When this psalm was written, Israel's capital city, Jerusalem, had already been sacked by the mighty Babylonians (in 586 BCE, about five hundred years after David). They destroyed the Temple and took many of the residents of Jerusalem captive to Babylon. Nebuchadnezzar, the Babylonian king who led the attack, blinded King Zedekiah and took him, bound and chained, back to Babylon, but not before slaughtering every one of Zedekiah's sons—the remaining descendants of David—replacing them with a non-Davidic puppet governor (2 Kings 25). It would be centuries before the Jews could even dream about restoring David's line and having a rightful king.

It looks like God—the Almighty Creator, who is steadfast and faithful—broke his promise about the never-ending line of David. Instead, despite the promise not to, God "spurned and rejected" (Psalm 89:38) David and his line by allowing the Babylonians to conquer Jerusalem. What happened to all the steadfastness of the promise-keeping Almighty Creator of the cosmos? Uh?

Now we know why the psalmist was piling on the compliments. He's backing God into a corner, accusing God with God's own words, perhaps playing on God's sense of honor that God is so quick to defend everywhere else. And with dripping sarcasm, the psalmist asks God, "How long, O LORD? Will you hide yourself *forever*?" (verse 46; emphasis added). Since God's promises clearly don't last forever, maybe his hiding will!

Things aren't as they should be, and God is at fault. God can't be counted on because God is a promise breaker. And this is in the Bible. How's that for spiritual guidance?

Actually, I think this is *great* for spiritual guidance. I love this uncomfortably real psalm. People of faith actually feel this way about God more often than they might be able to admit to friends and pastors. Maybe some of God's people today can relate to these words written about the same God 2,500 years ago.

No matter how well we think we know what God's next move *has* to be, things may not turn out that way. Remember that the writer of Psalm 89 had every reason to feel *certain* about what God's plan was: the Bible told him (in 2 Samuel 7). And yet things turned out differently. We should not be surprised when we find ourselves in a similar spot, experiencing a God who is not beholden to our thinking, a God who doesn't act according to our sense of certainty, even if we can find a Bible verse or two to back it up.

God can't be proof-texted. God will not be backed into a corner.

Yet even Psalm 89 ends (amazingly), "Blessed be the LORD forever. Amen and Amen" (verse 52). That line is actually the closing comment for Psalms 73–89, the third of five sections (or "books") of the Psalter. But perhaps, deep down, even now, the psalmist still *trusts God enough* to get in his face and call him a liar.

Even if we would never talk like this in church, I'm glad the Bible does. We need to hear it. At least I know I do.

# The World Makes Perfect Sense Without God

Another of my favorite God-is-not-coming-through-as-he-promised psalms is Psalm 73. If you've ever felt like you just don't see the point of all this believing in God business, this psalm is for you.

The psalm begins (verses 1–2):

> Truly God is good to the upright,
>     to those who are pure in heart.
> But as for me, my feet had almost stumbled;
>     my steps had nearly slipped.

The psalmist *knows* how things are supposed to work—"Truly" he says, which can also be translated, "No doubt." And this is what he knows: God blesses the righteous and punishes the wicked. So as long as you're righteous, God's blessings will be headed your way.

So what is this guy's problem? What made him almost stumble and slip? The theory, as good as it sounds, doesn't work because (once again) God doesn't follow through. In fact, the reverse happens: the wicked actually prosper while the righteous suffer.

> For I was envious of the arrogant;
>> I saw the prosperity of the wicked.
> For they have no pain;
>> their bodies are sound and sleek.
> They are not in trouble as others are;
>> They are not plagued like other people.
>
> (verses 3–5)

The psalmist is on a roll here, and he goes on for a few more verses, saying that the wicked not only prosper, but they also oppress the poor—and one of the very things Israel's God is supposed to be known for is protecting the down and out. And the wicked are even arrogant enough to "set their mouths against heaven" (verse 9). Yet God does nothing about it. Meanwhile, the righteous ones, like the psalmist, are sucking wind trying to make it through the day and can't catch a break; he is "plagued" and "punished every morning" (verse 14).

The issue for the psalmist isn't the mere fact that the wicked prosper. What sends him into crisis mode is that *God is letting the wicked prosper* when God had clearly laid down the law that the righteous will prosper and the wicked will be punished.

The psalmist didn't get this idea out of thin air. The book of Psalms opens up (Psalm 1) with a nice short let's-get-off-on-the-right-foot psalm about how the "righteous" ones (those who meditate on the Law of Moses and follow God's ways) are like "trees planted by streams of water" that never wither, but the "wicked" are "like chaff that the wind drives away" (verses 3–4). It's right there in writing.

This psalmist doesn't exactly call God a liar, as Psalm 89 does, but he is reminding God of his own words, wondering out loud, "If we have to obey what you say, why don't you?"

So why bother with you, God? The world makes just as good sense without you—maybe better, because without you hovering over my consciousness, I don't have to deal with the injustice of you not coming through on the plan you yourself put into action.

The thought of God not coming through, of God not being worthy of our trust, is so distressing that the psalmist is about to explode.

If I had said, "I will talk on in this way,"
  I would have been untrue to the circle of your children.
But when I thought how to understand this,
  it seemed to me a wearisome task.
(Psalm. 73:15–16)

He can't talk out loud about what he sees. If he did, he would have ruined other people's faith—sort of like pastors who have a crisis of faith but can't tell anyone about it. So they keep it inside, but that becomes a "wearisome task"—like carrying around a dead weight in their stomachs.

The world isn't working the way God said it does. "Good things happen to good people" is a nice idea to have in the Bible, but the real world tends to get in the way of our thinking that we are certain what God will do.

Parents know this by the time their child is two years old. You can read the right books and have a really good plan of attack for raising them to turn out "right," but then life happens: their own DNA comes to the surface, they interact with their environment, make friends, eventually go to day care and then school. Soon they start thinking and acting for themselves, and comparing your original ideal version with the actual offspring in front of you can be shocking.

Like parenting, faith in God doesn't follow a script—even if, as Psalm 73 shows us, that script is the Bible. The disconnect between how the psalmist thinks things should work and how his life actually turns out produces a crisis of faith. What he thought he knew, what he was so certain of, turned out not to work.

How does the psalmist's crisis play out at the end? He realizes that brooding isn't doing him any good, and so he enters "the sanctuary of God" (verse 17; to worship, maybe offer a sacrifice). There he sees that God can still be trusted because, one day, God will *eventually* come through and punish the wicked. After all, God only said the wicked will be punished. God never said when. Trusting God calls for patience. In the meantime, I'm sure the psalmist is clearing out his schedule so he can make regular visits to the Temple to ask God how much longer this is going to take.

What keeps the psalmist going here is the knowledge that one day the wicked will get what's coming to them. The psalmist sees God as retributive, paying back the bad guys (who might even be fellow Israelites!) fairly and swiftly, in this life (not in the afterlife), through some physical punishment (like death, plague, war, hunger, exile).

Waiting and hoping for this sort of divine retribution is common in the Psalms and elsewhere in the Bible. No one reading this today, however, should feel like they ought to pray to God like this. For

Christians, praying for this sort of divine retribution is completely off the table—Jesus said we are to pray for those who persecute us (Matthew 5:43–48).

So we need to focus here less on what the psalmist wants to see happen to the bad guys and more on what he *does*.

Even when all the evidence showed that God doesn't follow through on the rules, the psalmist *enters the sanctuary;* he moves *toward* God, not away from God—*a movement toward trust when all the evidence is against it.* That was the only option open to him.

When my wife, Sue, has an issue with me (a purely hypothetical situation, since I am a flawless husband), I appreciate when she comes to me with the problem rather than talking about me to a friend, her sisters, or her mother. A relationship based on trust means not walking on eggshells, but talking openly, honestly, with no hint of passive-aggressiveness or any of the other dysfunctional manipulative tactics we tend to impose on family and friends.

After a period of brooding to himself, entering the sanctuary was the psalmist's act of trust. That's the take-home message here for us.

Our psalmists wouldn't make very good Christian fundamentalists, who see the Bible as a source of certain knowledge about God, the world, and our place in it. Rather these psalmists are laying it all in front of us, that the Bible is less an instructional manual and more of an internal dialogue, even debate, among people of faith about just who this God is they are dealing with. For them, certainty about God had exploded before their eyes. But even when they had no logical reason to trust God, they pushed through and trusted God *anyway.* Even when they thought of God as a neglectful parent or liar.

I'm beginning to understand a bit more, now in my middle-aged years, that trust in God grows best when things are falling apart; or as the seventeenth-century Scottish theologian Samuel Rutherford said, "Grace grows best in winter." Some pilgrims live in February.

I think these psalmists and a couple of other miserable characters in the Bible would agree.

# Two Miserable People Worth Listening To

I am poured out like water, and all my bones are out of joint;
my heart is like wax; it is melted within my breast.

—Psalm 22:14

# Trust God Anyway

If faith in God makes zero sense to you and reasons for trusting God have fallen off a cliff of despair, you've got a friend in the Bible: the book of Ecclesiastes. This book goes even further than the psalms we looked at. Not only can God not be counted on, but life plays out as one cruel joke after another, and then you die.

And God is to blame.

> It is an unhappy business that God has given to human
> beings to be busy with. I saw all the deeds that are
> done under the sun; and see, all is vanity and a
> chasing after wind.
> What is crooked cannot be made straight,
> and what is lacking cannot be counted.
> (Ecclesiastes 1:13–15; see also 7:13)

These are the words of the main speaker of the book, the otherwise unknown Qohelet—aka the "Teacher" or "Preacher" as some Bible translations have it. No one really knows what the name means, but *Teacher* or *Preacher* definitely don't do justice to his alarming point of view.

As we can see, Qohelet has serious issues with God. Our lives down here ("under the sun," as he puts it) are full of "unhappy business" that God has "given" us. Our day-to-day deeds get us nowhere, like "chasing after wind." God set up the world like that! And we can't do anything to change it—what God has done is "crooked" and can't be straightened, "lacking" and can't be "counted."

And this is in the Bible.

Qohelet is in major faith-crisis mode. All signs indicate to him that God has orchestrated an absurd existence for us humans, as futile as the cycles of nature (1:5–10). Just think of the poor old sun, Qohelet tells us. It rises and sets every day without a rest, again . . . and again . . . and again . . . with nothing to show for it, no progress made, no payday waiting at the end. Or consider the wind. It blows this way and that, round and round in a never-ending, meaningless, futile, tedious cycle. The streams, too, never stop flowing into the sea, yet the sea never fills up. All that effort, but it makes zero difference.

Just like nature, humans run around in circles, working hard day in and day out, with ultimately nothing to show for it—because at the end, we all die.

*That* is Qohelet's major issue, the hump he can't get over and what is causing him all his pain. Death neutralizes all our toil. We can spend the years of our lives accomplishing great things, making a truckload of money, and owning half of Manhattan, but we can't take it with us.

Of course, we all die, so what's Qohelet getting all worked up about? Well, it's just that: we all die. And then we are quickly forgotten as if we never were, just like we've forgotten already those who lived and died before us.

> The people of long ago are not remembered,
>    nor will there be any remembrance
> of people yet to come
>    by those who come after them.
> (1:11)

Quite the buzzkill, this Qohelet. Not one to try out for the cheerleading squad. But he's got a point.

Think of the mass of humanity that has gone before us over the last century. We don't know who 99.99999 percent of them even were enough to forget them. And those we've heard of, like Princess Di, Michael Jackson, and Robin Williams, pass by and slip from our memories as quickly as our Facebook news feeds scroll past us and disappear. We go on living, for all practical purposes, having forgotten them completely unless reminded.

Old friends, roommates, or coworkers will linger longer and come to mind more often—but how often? Does it not often take some accidental reminder amid our busy lives to recall those who are no longer here—even those closest to us? Are they not also, for all practical purposes, forgotten?

As this book goes to print, my parents died seven and ten years ago. I have to admit, I don't think of them every day, and in all likelihood, my grandchildren and great-grandchildren will think of them even less—if at all. Heck, my descendants won't even think of me, just as I hardly ever remember my grandparents. And I don't even know my great-grandparents' names, at least not without doing some digging.

Qohelet really does have a point. We're so busy hyperventilating on the go-nowhere hamster wheel that we don't have space to keep the dead in our active memories. Nor do we take the time to ponder our own mortality. Life is one big hurried distraction to find "meaning," but in the end, we die regardless, and then we're forgotten.

And don't try telling Qohelet "There, there, my lad. Not to worry. After we die, we go to heaven, and then everything will be okay and everything will make sense." Qohelet is skeptical,

> For the fate of humans and the fate of animals is the same;
> as one dies, so dies the other. They all have the same breath,
> and humans have no advantage over the animals; for all is
> vanity. All go to one place; all are from the dust, and all
> turn to dust again. Who knows whether the human spirit
> goes upward and the spirit of animals goes downward to the
> earth? (Ecclesiastes 3:19–21)

I wonder how many invitations Qohelet would get to speak at fundraisers or funerals. Don't let anyone tell you the Bible is all happy-clappy.

Qohelet looked life square in the eye and refused to play the religion game, where everything is working out and God makes sense. I'm drawn to his honesty and the fact that he is saying what we all feel, at least now and then.

Don't get me wrong. I'm not suggesting that we dive in with Qohelet and try to live lives of despair, glorifying our doubt. I'm not even suggesting that he has the last word. But I *am* suggesting we pay attention to what this book is saying *through* Qohelet's despair—which is where the book ends. There we see a startling lesson of faith, a faith that has let go of needing to know.

After twelve chapters, with hardly a break to lighten up the mood, Qohelet's voice ends and a narrator takes over (12:9–14; he also introduced Qohelet in the opening verses of the book). Remarkably, he doesn't reprimand Qohelet for his lack of solid faith or try to get God off the hook. He just leaves it there. In fact, he tells us, despite Qohelet's Eeyore vibe, that Qohelet is *wise* and a teacher of *knowledge*. Qohelet's words are not brushed aside with a sigh of relief. They are worth hearing, even though they are painful to hear:

The sayings of the wise are like goads, and like nails firmly fixed are the collected sayings that are given by one shepherd. (12:11)

Wise words hurt—like a shepherd's goad, a long staff with a nail at the end used to prod the sheep. The narrator has no intention of taming the previous twelve chapters. Qohelet's words hurt. They are supposed to.

But the narrator continues. Even though Qohelet's words are wise, we are not to live in that same space perpetually, brooding about life, rehashing it all over and over again:

Of making many books there is no end, and much study is a weariness of the flesh. The end of the matter; all has been heard. Fear God, and keep his commandments; for that is the whole duty of everyone. (12:12–13)

The narrator isn't telling his audience to stop reading books (as much as my college students would like to hear that). He means obsessing and trying to work it all out is spiritually and emotionally exhausting. And so, "Stop it." No more words. Nothing more needs to be said.

What remains is not a plunge off the cliff of despair—even though who could blame anyone at this point?—but the opposite: fear God (revere and respect God) and keep God's commandments.

The book of Ecclesiastes doesn't mask the reality but neither does that reality have the final word. Keep being a faithful Israelite *anyway*. Continue on fearing and obeying God *anyway*. Reverence and obedience have *always been and still are* the mark of a faithful Israelite.

Nothing changes that, even the belief that all of this God business is futile and senseless. Even when life is absurd and only death waits for us at the other end. Even then we still read, "Yes. I get it. I've been there. We all get there sooner or later. And when you do, keep on being an Israelite *anyway*. Fear God and live obediently before God *anyway*."

Anyway.

I don't say that lightly. It's hard to keep trusting God when you see no reason to. Yet that is a profound paradox of faith in the book of Ecclesiastes. No matter how deep distrust and disillusionment may be, move toward God in trust *anyway*.

When we reach that point where things simply make no sense, when our thinking about God and life no longer line up, when any sense of certainty is gone, and when we can find *no* reason to trust God *but we still do*, well, that is what trust looks like at its brightest—when all else is dark.

The book of Ecclesiastes isn't a drawn-out and sorry tale of weak faith and poor thinking that the truly faithful need to avoid. It is an honest reflection of what people of true faith experience. The author drags his readers through one discouraging scenario after another, where reasonable people might give up. But if we stay around for the end, we may discover some of the more encouraging words in the entire Bible:

> Face it all head on, with complete transparency and
> unflinching honesty, without making excuses for yourself or
> God . . . and trust God anyway.

Ecclesiastes is one of the true gems of the Bible. It paints for us a picture of what faith looks like when *all* you thought you knew about God and how the world works is ripped from you, when certainty vanishes like a vapor.

I spent my college summers using jackhammers and digging holes for a public-utilities company. Now and then, I would speak of my faith with a rather gruff foreman. At one point, he said (and I'll leave out his more colorful "sentence enhancers," as SpongeBob calls them), "You know, Pete, a guy who really believes all that . . . well . . . you can't *kill* a guy like that."

So true. When we have stared into the pit of despair over God and his world, and our thoughts about God don't line up at all, and then we trust God *anyway*, enough to continue living in the hope that trusting God is worth it—even just the faint hope of having hope—well, you can't kill someone like that.

Ecclesiastes never says "You gotta know what you believe," but rather "Trust God even when you don't know what you believe, even when all before you is absurd."

# Don't Even *Try* to Understand What God Is Up To

And then there's Job, the most miserable person in the Bible. Though it's not his fault. Like the psalms we looked at, God doesn't act toward Job as one might expect.

Job's life was flowing right along like a country stream (Job 1). He was a family man, a father of ten, and had livestock and riches like no one else, which is biblical shorthand for "blessed by God." Job was also deeply devout. After family get-togethers, Job would offer some sacrifices to God just on the off chance his children may have sinned. If anyone was doing it right, it was Job.

So far so good, but we are taken quickly to a heavenly scene where Israel's God, Yahweh, is holding court while other "heavenly beings" present themselves to him. Just who these heavenly beings are isn't clear, but elsewhere in the Bible we read of Israel's God presiding over a council of divine beings (Psalm 82), so that's the basic idea here, too. One of these divine beings, who presents himself to Yahweh, is called *ha-satan* (hah-sah-TAHN). Most Bibles give him the name Satan, which is unfortunate because it conjures up the red tights and pitchfork of God's archenemy, a creation of medieval Christian theology. *Ha-satan* isn't "Satan" but a title, "the Accuser"—like a prosecuting attorney.

The Accuser, a divine being, had just gotten back from doing an inspection run of the earth, and God starts bragging about how no one on Earth is as blameless and upright as his "servant Job." The Accuser isn't impressed. He's dead sure that the only reason Job is so devout is because Yahweh is hovering over him like a helicopter parent, blessing him with family and riches. He accuses Job of worshiping Yahweh because of what's in it for him. So he bets Yahweh that if he were to remove his blessing from Job, Job's devotion would fold like a cheap card table and he would be found out for the superficial God worshipper he is.

Amazingly, Yahweh *takes the bet*! And with that, the rest of the book unfolds. Yahweh tells the Accuser to have at it, the only stipulation being he needs to stop short of killing Job. But everything up to that is fair game.

The Accuser can't wait to get started. In short order, Job's livestock are stolen or killed along with his servants, and a wind blows a house down on top of his children, killing all ten. After a second audience with Yahweh (Job 2), the Accuser is given permission yet a second time to go back down and smite Job himself with sores from head to toe, all of which prompts Job, understandably, to curse the day his parents conceived him (Job 3). He also wonders what in the world God is doing to him.

Job's three friends have been watching all this—and he is such a mess they hardly recognize him. At first, they sit down by his side for seven days and nights without saying a word, tearing their robes and heaping ashes on their heads as signs of mourning. These are good friends to have. After seven days, the three friends (who are later joined by a fourth) begin to talk to Job, which leads to a very long series of speeches where they each take turns trying to get Job to see that he must have done something to deserve this.

Whether or not Job wants to hear it, his friends—being good, honest, tough-love kinds of friends—tell Job that God must be punishing him for something he did. There can be no other explanation. God is just, after all, and does not punish on a flaky whim (like taking a bet?!). Likewise, Job's friend, Bildad, says his children must have been killed because *they* sinned and deserved it (Job 8:4). To make his own suffering stop, Job simply needs to do what everyone knows you have to do in a situation like this: repent of his sin.

But Job isn't so sure about that. At times, he says, "Yeah, I get your point, but why doesn't God tell me what I did, because I have no clue?!" But he quickly shifts over to "But I *didn't do* anything wrong?!" This back and forth between Job ("I'm innocent") and his friends ("No you're not") carries on for thirty-four chapters, each side of the argument getting plenty of airtime.

Of course, readers of the book of Job know all about the bet, even though Job and his friends don't, so we know Job really *is* innocent. In fact, in light of that bit of knowledge we have, Job's friends start sounding like annoying spiritual know-it-alls who claim to have God all figured out.

But let's not be too hard on Job's friends. They aren't aware of the bet. Based on what they *do* know, they've got a good point. "You must have done something to deserve it" is a mainstream biblical idea: actions have consequences.

In the book of Proverbs, for example, being wise and obedient leads to blessing and a life in harmony with God, but foolishness and disobedience lead to bad consequences. From beginning to end, Proverbs drives home the idea that the choices we make, whether wise or foolish, lead somewhere.

> The LORD's curse is on the house of the wicked,
>> but he blesses the abode of the righteous.
> Toward the scorners he is scornful,
>> but to the humble he shows favor.
> The wise will inherit honor,
>> but stubborn fools, disgrace.
> (Proverbs 3:33–35)

Job's friends are simply trying to get this perfectly normal, biblical idea across to him. Job is obviously cursed, scorned, and disgraced, and so "What did you do?" is a perfectly reasonable question to ask of him.

In fact the "actions have consequences" idea also explains Israel's entire national epic—why the Israelites were removed from the Promised Land and taken into exile in Babylon. Over and over again we read how Israel's disobedience to God's law led directly to disastrous consequences. The whole scheme is laid out for us in black and white in the book of Deuteronomy, chapter 28, where Moses gives the people one last pep talk before entering the land of Canaan. The message is basically this:

> If you obey God, things will go very, very, very well for you
> in the Promised Land. The fruit of your womb and the fruit
> of the land will be plenty, you'll have all the rain you need,
> and your enemies won't touch you—you will be blessed.

But if you disobey, things will go horribly, miserably, badly wrong for you. You'll face a laundry list of misery: disease, drought, starvation, childlessness, and your enemies will take you captive and others will move into your land—you will be cursed.

God puts before the Israelites a crucial choice, whether to live a life of obedience or disobedience, and the choice they make will have definite consequences—you can count on it because God says so.

And so we find Job experiencing some consequence of his own. In fact, one of those consequences is that he has sores "from the sole of his foot to the crown of his head" (Job 2:7). It doesn't help Job's case for innocence that God promises the disobedient Israelites, in Deuteronomy, that he will strike them with boils: "from the sole of your foot to the crown of your head" (Deuteronomy 28:35).

Let's put ourselves in the place of Job's friends who took seriously this biblical view of actions and consequences and of God as someone who treats people according to their actions. They pay their friend Job a visit, see the state he's in, and draw the only conclusion we can expect—that Job must have done something to incur God's wrath. Yet Job is perplexed, and Job's friends are perplexed that he is perplexed.

Furthermore, as his friends remind him, Job has been benefiting from God's blessing for a long time. He even used to teach others how the actions-consequences idea works. But now, when he is the one suffering, all of a sudden he has no idea what's going on? How quickly Job has forgotten! Where is his integrity?

And so his friends are well within their right—in fact it is their responsibility—to talk some sense into Job by reminding him of all those things he himself already "knows" about how God works.

Job understands the theory, which is precisely his problem—he has no idea why God has painted a "target" on his back and why God himself has shot him full of "arrows" (see Job 7:20 and 6:4). And so Job is in full crisis mode because he has nowhere to turn, no one who will uphold his innocence before God—no one to confront God with why God is acting so un-Godlike.

> Does it seem good to you to oppress,
>> to despise the work of your hands
>> and favor the schemes of the wicked?
> Do you have eyes of flesh?
>> Do you see as humans see?
> Are your days like the days of mortals,
>> or your years like human years,
> that you seek out my iniquity
>> and search for my sin,
> although you know that I am not guilty,
>> and there is no one to deliver out of your hand?
> (Job 10:3–7)

In other words, "God, why are you acting like a mere mortal toward me—and an unjust mortal at that—looking for my sins even when you know I am innocent?"

Just like the book of Ecclesiastes, this long back and forth between Job and his friends isn't just a lot of filler material to say, "Here's one big example of what unfaithfulness looks like. Don't do that." Rather, the dialogue is drawn out to explore from different angles the very real and common idea we have seen in the Psalms and Ecclesiastes:

What we know or think we know about God might not be
so certain, no matter how absolutely certain we think we
are—no matter how certain we might even think we have the
right to be.

And again, that holds true even if our sense of certainty comes
from the Bible. Yes, sometimes the biblical writers present God's ways
in absolute black and white. But even if you are able to quote chapter
and verse, don't count on these portraits of God to work everywhere
and every time. The Bible isn't a Christian owner's manual. God
remains shrouded in mystery, inaccessible, beyond our mental reach.

Which is precisely what God says when he finally inserts himself
into the conversation.

Over the course of the last four chapters (38–42), God makes
it clear that he isn't impressed with longwinded speeches. God lays
out the case that he, and only he, is the Creator, and therefore, these
mortals are in no position to question him.

I have to say, I've never completely gotten on board with God's
answer. Job wasn't asking a philosophical question, "Why do bad
things happen to good people?" or even "Why are bad things happening to me?" Rather, he was asking, as were the authors of the
Psalms, "My life is leaking out of me. Why aren't you true to your
own promises? If we have to play by your rules, Oh Lord, why don't
you?"

God could easily have told Job about the bet with the Accuser.
But no—it's like God doesn't want Job to know what transpired in
that heavenly dialogue. Rather Yahweh gives a rather long-winded
speech of his own about how he is the Creator, and since Job isn't,
he has no right to stand there and interrogate God. Job fires back—

and these are his last words in the book (42:1–6)—that he knows how great and powerful God is, but he'd still like an answer to the question that has been plaguing him (pun intentional) since chapter 3: "Why is all this happening to me when I didn't do anything to deserve it?"

Job does not back down and accept Yahweh's four-chapter filibuster. He stands firm in his effort to get an answer from Yahweh. It is *this* resolution of Job's, to be honest in his confrontation with God rather than take unjust punishment, that leads Yahweh to say to Job's friend Eliphaz,

> My wrath is kindled against you and against your two
> friends; for you have not spoken of me what is right,
> as my servant Job has. (42:7)

So after all the "don't question me because I'm God" business, God tells all who have been rooting for Job what they've been waiting to hear: Job was right, and his friends were wrong.

Job's friends were technically right *if you're going by the book*. They had every reason to feel certain about why Job was suffering. But God says they are wrong.

Job and his friends were operating under the same assumption that God wants humans to know, and indeed has made known, the basic pattern of reality—that is, what God expects from them and the basic rules for living. Job never denies this way of thinking, which is precisely what causes him so much distress—he can't square his suffering with his "biblical" view of how God works.

So here is another book of the Bible that tells us to let go of the need to know—better, of the expectation that we *can* know the inner workings of God. However sure and true we think our thoughts about God might be, struggling with God in the here and now may never be far away, challenging what we "know"—even if that knowledge comes straight out the Bible, chapter and verse.

When we come to our own Job-like moments, the way forward isn't to expect God to give us some additional piece of information to make everything fall into place. The answer that people like Job and his friends want—because they've got to "know what they believe"—is precisely the answer God keeps hidden. No special bit of knowledge for you.

Rather, God exposes the limitations of our thinking. Then we can see the inevitability to letting go of the need to know and trust God instead—as best as we can each moment—because God is God.

Trust like this is an affront to reason, the control our egos crave. Which is precisely the point. Trust does not work because we have captured God in our minds. It works regardless of the fact that, at the end of the day, we finally learn that we can't.

# Believing in God: So Easy Even a Demon Can Do It

And those who know your name put their trust in you,
for you, O Lord, have not forsaken those who seek you.

—Psalm 9:10

# *Who,* Not *What*

Some of you might be thinking, Okay, I get it with some psalms, Ecclesiastes, and Job, but those guys are hardly mainstream. They're even a bit flakey. Isn't the heart of the Bible big on knowing what you believe? Doesn't the Bible tell us how important it is to "believe" the right things about God?

I definitely get where these questions are coming from, and remember: I don't think "knowing" or seeking to think "correctly" about God is *wrong.* Not at all. The problem is *preoccupation* with correct thinking—mistaking our thoughts about God with the real thing, and then to base our faith on holding on to that certainty.

The Bible is not remotely interested in that preoccupation.

Which brings me to a little problem with the word *believe* (and *belief*).

Think of how we use the word *believe* when we talk about our faith: "*What* do you believe in? Really? I don't believe in *that* at all. Here's *what* I believe. Boy, *what* you believe and *what* I believe are very different. You couldn't join my church or date my daughter with beliefs like *that.*"

"What" and "that." Almost as a reflex, *believing* is a "thinking" word, a word to describe the content of our thoughts: I believe *that* God exists (and atheists don't believe that), I believe *that* God created the world (not random chance), I believe *that* Jesus is God's Son (and not just another Jewish carpenter), and so on. Church creeds and ten-point statements of faith emphasize content, thoughts about God to be listed and agreed with.

I'm not against creeds or talking about what I believe. But as it's used in the Bible, *believing* doesn't focus on *what* someone believes in, but *in whom* one places his or her *trust*—namely God.

*Believing* is a "who" word.

If we forget that, we will read into the Bible our own tendency to put *what* at the heart of *belief*, which sets us up to be preoccupied with correct thinking. And that misses the point.

Of course, *believing* is never empty of content. The Israelites trusted God *because* of what God had done for them, namely delivering the Israelites from harm (Egyptian slavery and Babylonian captivity being the two big examples). But when we come across the idea of *believing* in the Bible, the focus isn't on *what* but *who*. Not content of thinking, but trust in a person. That's the main point I am making here.

People in biblical times, after all, simply didn't have the same preoccupation with *what* to believe as modern people do. For us, any religion, including Christianity, faces intellectual challenges that weren't on anyone's radar screens a few millennia ago. Does the heavenly divine realm actually exist? was not a pressing question of the day (though I'm sure skeptics could be found).

In fact, the divine realm did more than simply exist; it was the ultimate reality by which the mundane here-and-now world was explained. The writer of Ecclesiastes comes close to the exception—his skepticism screwed him into the ground so far he was ready to pack it all in. But, like Job and Psalms, his issue was really why God is no longer trustworthy, or why it even mattered, and not whether or not God and the divine realm are real.

Today, skepticism and disbelief in a divine realm are common, a live option for many—almost a norm that doesn't need explaining, at least in Western culture. A bright, college-educated, twentysomething woman said to me not long ago, "The more you know, the harder it is to believe in God." She meant that our modern world explains things quite compellingly in scientific rather than supernatural means, which makes it harder to believe that God exists—or at least the personal God in the Bible, looking down from a heavenly throne.

So when we see "belief" or "believe" in the Bible, tempting though it may be, we shouldn't transport our overly intellectualized meaning onto biblical characters. If we replace these words with *trust*, we'll be closer to what the Bible is getting at. And we may be surprised, and encouraged, at what we see.

# Amen

Early in the Bible, in the book of Genesis, we read of father Abraham, the patriarch of what would become the Israelites. As the story goes, God appears to Abraham (called Abram at this point) in a vision. God promises Abraham that, although childless and getting on in years, he and his wife Sarah (Sarai) would in time have a son (Isaac), and eventually, his descendants would be as uncountable as the stars in the sky.

We can safely chalk this up to the kind of overstatement we find in the Bible when it comes to numbers, but that's not the point. We are told that, in response to this promise, Abraham "believed the LORD" (Genesis 15:6)—which is the first place in the Bible where believing comes up.

*Believe* in the original Hebrew of this story is *'aman* (ah-MAHN), which has made its way into English, and we all know it as *amen*—only, it's not a social cue that we're done praying, and it's okay to open our eyes and dig in. *Amen* as the final word of a prayer is a declaration of trust: "We're done talking now, Lord. We've said our peace and put this matter into your hands. Now we trust you with it."

God promised a very old man and his very old and barren wife a lot of kids. And Abraham believed—not simply *that* God was able to pull it off, but he trusted God *to* pull it off. Abraham "amened" God to come through. Of course, it's absolutely fine to say that Abraham "believed," but only if we control our reflex to push that word into the "what/that" category of our thinking *about* God and remember it is a "who" word of trust *in* God.

"Belief" shows up in the New Testament a lot, and it's a trust word there, too. Like when a man brought his son, who was convulsing and foaming at the mouth, to Jesus for healing (Mark 9:14–29). Jesus said, "All things can be done for the one who believes" (9:23). To which the father cried out, "I believe; help my unbelief!"

Of course, as we all know, this suffering father isn't saying, "Jesus, I am operating on about an 85 percent degree of certainty that you are able to do this, but I'd like you to rev it up to 100 percent." Rather—as I think most any parent can understand—the father needs help letting go. The situation is out of his control. He needs to trust Jesus with his son. The man says in effect, "Yes, I trust you. I'm trying, at least. I want to. I'm scared. Help me to trust you."

Or there's the story of Jesus arriving too late to heal the daughter of Jairus, a leader of the synagogue (Luke 8:40–56). While Jesus is delayed, word comes to him that the girl has already died and so not to bother coming. Jesus replies, "Do not fear. Only believe, and she will be saved" (8:50). Jesus arrives at the house, but the thought of doing anything to help the girl now was utterly irrational. When Jesus said, "Only believe," he was clearly asking them, and Jairus especially, to trust him to come through—to entrust his daughter to him.

The book of James summarizes the idea in one verse: "You believe that God is one; you do well. Even the demons believe—and shudder" (James 2:19; emphasis added). Believing *that* God is *x, y,* or *z* has its place, but it is so easy even a demon can do it. Moving from your head to your whole self, however, where your belief is all in—where you *trust* God—well, that is something else entirely. And that's the part we can't lose sight of when we talk about believing.

*Believing* is a "who" word—letting go of fear and the burning impulse to act, and trusting God. So when I come across that word in the Bible, I replace it with *trust,* and it always makes a big difference. I'm challenged to get out of my head, where I'm warm and safe, and feel the risk of trusting God.

Believing is easy. It gives us wiggle room to think our way out of a tight spot. But trust doesn't have any wiggle room. It explodes it. Trust is about being all in.

# Faith Isn't Something
# in Your Head (or Heart)

When we say that someone "has faith," we run into a similar problem as with "belief." We might say to someone, "Tell me about your faith," and the answer we get might be something like, "Well, I'm a Christian. I believe that Jesus is the Son of God, who died for my sins," and so on.

Again, nothing wrong with that. *Faith,* like *belief,* includes content—the *what*—but again, we can't stay on that level. If we do, we're going to miss out on a lot. We see "faith" throughout the New Testament, and it's typically not about the content of what to think. It's about trusting God—*and acting on it.*

*Faith* is a *who* word, a trust word. We've just seen two examples of it in the stories of the father with the sick son and Jairus's dead daughter: "I believe; help my unbelief" and "Only believe, and she will be saved."

I know these passages say "unbelief" and "believe," but the Greek word behind it is the same one translated as "faith" elsewhere in the

New Testament: *pistis* (PIS-tis). So even though in English we see two different words, in Greek they are one and the same with two different uses.

Grammar lesson aside, we just need to be alert to what's happening when we see "believe" or "faith" in the New Testament: these are about all-in trust, not something we believe about God or Jesus.

*Pistis* is also an action word—and here is where things get interesting. When used as an action word, *pistis* is usually translated as faithful/faithfulness or trustworthy/trustworthiness.

So what? Well, knowing this will give us a bigger and deeper view of what the New Testament writers are after when they talk about faith. And it's not so much something we "have," like the thoughts we "have" in our heads or the feelings we "have" in our hearts.

*Faith* describes our whole way of looking at life and how we act on that.

*Faith* describes a parent letting go of the fear for his child and handing that child over to Jesus. Faith like that is a conscious decision to trust—and it's hard to let go of control and do that. *Faith* is a tough word.

Faith is not only directed toward God but toward other people. Followers of Jesus are to be *pistis* toward each other—meaning "faithful" toward each other. As Paul puts it, " . . . the only thing that counts is faith [*pistis*] working through love" (Galatians 5:6). He isn't saying, "Listen, we've got two things going on here: the faith we have *inside* and then the love we show toward others." Replacing "faith" with *faithfulness* helps us see Paul's point more clearly. He is saying that faith and love are two sides of the same coin.

Faith isn't simply something that happens between God and us. *Faith* is a community word.

One of Paul's favorite ways for summing up faithfulness toward one other is humility: the attitude and act of putting others before our own wants and desires. "Do nothing from selfish ambition or conceit, but in humility regard others as better than yourselves" (Philippians 2:3). That in a nutshell is *pistis*.

But there's more.

*Faith* also describes what *God* does—which is a big clue that "having faith" doesn't quite cut it. God doesn't "have faith," but God is *faithful*. How? We see God's faithfulness by what God does.

We saw this already in Psalm 89. Again and again, the psalmist writes of God's steadfast love and faithfulness (*'aman*). Remember, the complaint of Psalm 89 was that God was all talk and no action. Promises are fine, but only if God actually does something— preserve David's line of descendants. If not then God isn't faithful, no matter what God says.

Likewise in Psalm 40, David praises God for delivering him from some threat:

I have not hidden your saving help within my heart,
    I have spoken of your faithfulness [*'aman*] and your
        salvation.
(verse 10)

In the New Testament, God's steadfast love and faithfulness are seen, not in an act of deliverance from foreign enemies, but in sending the Son and raising him from the dead to enact a global rescue mission (Romans 8:3).

Jesus is God's supreme, grand, climactic act of faithfulness.

Not only that, but *faithful* also describes Jesus. Paul writes,

. . . we know that a person is justified not by the works of
the law but through *faith in Jesus Christ.* (Galatians 2:16;
emphasis added)

A better reading is "*faithfulness of* Jesus Christ" (which is found
in footnotes of many Bibles), and the two readings couldn't be more
different. (And I have a rather long note explaining this in the back
of the book.)

Paul isn't saying, "You are not justified before God by your
efforts, but by *your* faith." The contrast he's making isn't between
two options *we* have. The contrast is between *your* efforts and *Jesus's
faithfulness to* you—shown in his obedient death on a Roman cross.
Paul is interested in telling readers about what *Jesus did,* about Jesus's
faithfulness, not what we do.

God's grand act of faithfulness is giving his only Son for our
sake. God is all in.

Jesus's grand act of faithfulness is going through with it for our
sake. Jesus is all in.

Now it's our move, which really is the point of all this.

Like God the Father and God the Son, we are also called to be
faithful. On one level, we are faithful to God when we trust God.
But faith—*pistis*—doesn't stop there. It extends, as we've seen, to
faithfulness toward each other—in humility and self-sacrificial love.

And here is the real kick in the pants. When we are faithful to each
other like this, we are more than simply being nice and kind, though
there's that. Far more important, when we are faithful to each other,
we are at that moment *acting like the faithful God and the faithful Son.*

Being like God. That's the goal. And we are most like God not
when we are certain we are right about God, or when we tell others

how right we are, but when we are acting toward one another like the faithful Father and Son.

Humility, love, and kindness are *our* grand acts of faithfulness and how we show that we are all in. "No one has ever seen God; if we love one another, God lives in us, and his love is perfected in us" (1 John 4:12). Loving each other is the closest we get to seeing God.

Being "in" with God is about much more than the thoughts we keep in our heads, the belief systems we hold on to, the doctrines we recite, or the statements of faith we adhere to, no matter how fervently and genuinely we do so, and how important they may be. Being obsessed with making sure we have all our thoughts about God properly arranged and defended isn't faith. How trusting we are of God day to day and how Godlike we live among those around us day to day is.

As the book of James puts it, a faith without actions is dead—without value:

> What good is it, my brothers and sisters, if you say you have faith but do not have works? Can faith save you? If a brother or sister is naked and lacks daily food, and one of you says to them, "Go in peace; keep warm and eat your fill," and yet you do not supply their bodily needs, what is the good of that? So faith by itself, if it has no works, is dead. But someone will say, "You have faith and I have works." Show me your faith apart from your works, and I by my works will show you my faith. (James 2:14–18)

We miss what the biblical writers were after if we think of *belief* and *faith* as "correct thinking" words. They are deep and hard words, more than we might have been led to expect. And they are beautiful words that move us deeper into the presence of God.

# "*All* to Jesus I Surrender"

"Trust God no matter what" is a big idea throughout the Bible—whether you're a nonagenarian couple and God promised you a child, a psalmist looking to God for deliverance, or a parent entrusting to God a dying child. But trusting God isn't just for when the chips are down and we're bunkered in a foxhole. Trusting God is for every moment, the normal state of those who say they believe.

This idea is driven home in a demanding yet also quietly comforting portion of the book of Proverbs.

> Trust in the LORD with all your heart,
>     and do not rely on your own insight.
> In all your ways acknowledge him,
>     and he will make straight your paths.
> (Proverbs 3:5–6)

In the Old Testament, "heart" isn't simply where the emotions reside. It's also the seat of one's thoughts, moral compass, and will. "With all your heart" means "all of you, every part of you—what you feel, think, do, and will."

Trusting God with all our hearts is a complete surrender, a life decision to be all in all the time rather than relying on our own "insight," our ability to understand, to fathom, to solve, to figure out. Trust remains when our reason betrays us, when we *don't* understand the mysteries of God and faith, when we don't see what God is up to—including when God for all intents and purposes is not faithful or trustworthy.

Our level of insight does not determine our level of trust. In fact, seeking insight rather than trust can get in the way of our walk with God.

Just ask Adam and Eve. When tempted by the serpent to eat the fruit from the forbidden tree of *knowledge* (Genesis 3), Eve would have done us all a favor by taking a step back and asking herself who in this transaction is worthy of her *trust*—her Creator or the crafty serpent. But instead, she reached for knowledge, for insight, and the result was a rather serious rupture of their relationship with God. Insight was gained—they knew they were naked—but at a price.

The Adam and Eve story is about what happens when knowing is elevated above trusting.

Trusting God isn't simply something to do in crisis, but "in all your ways"—even when we think we can figure things out, when we feel on top of the world because our theology and our experience are on the same page, and when God and our world make perfect sense (unlike Qohelet, Job, and our psalmists). Even then—precisely then—we should not slip into thinking that we actually do have a handle on it all, that we can "rely" on whatever insight we have.

"To rely" in Hebrew suggests "leaning" or "supporting oneself." Great concept. When I lean back in my sofa while watching ESPN, I don't give a thought to whether the cushions will be there and whether they will keep me from falling through the sofa and onto the floor. When I lean against a tree or wall, it never enters my mind that the oak or drywall aren't up for the task and might give way.

As I'm typing this I am leaning back against my chair, and the thought never enters my mind. You're probably leaning back against something right now, too. We are, in effect, trusting these objects right now without a care in the world.

Only God is worthy of that kind of all-in lean, that kind of trust. Our own insights are not worthy. They come and go and never apprehend the true breadth and depth of reality.

Again, leaning on God isn't just for the challenges, but also the moment-to-moment life we live, where we tend not to give much thought to God and God's ways. Spiritual maturity is living a God-conscious existence of being aware of the responsibility to choose whether we are going to trust God with all our moments, or trust ourselves.

After all, it's the little things that get to us, isn't it? When Sue and I were first married and I was in seminary and then graduate school, we had no money. If we had twenty dollars left over, we bought pizza. That was the extent of our budgeting. If it weren't for scholarships and help from parents and friends, I'm not sure how we would have made it —in fact, looking back, I'm not sure how it was that we didn't wind up living in a cardboard box on the sidewalk.

But we were happy and essentially worry free. That began to change slowly after I got my Ph.D. and took my first teaching job. Over time—about three to five years—my attitude had changed about money. We bought a house right out of graduate school, our three children took music lessons and played soccer, and I had home repairs, life insurance, and real estate taxes.

I remember standing in my living room when it finally hit me how I had changed over the last few years. Nothing big happened. Life had just snuck up on me slowly, bit by bit. Things had been going comparatively well, which fooled me into thinking, "Thanks, Creator of the universe, I'll take it from here"—never consciously, but just deep enough under the surface that I didn't realize what was happening. Looking back, I was very good at the "Lord, deliver me" part of faith but not the "in all your ways" part. I'm still working on it.

Hence, "In *all* your ways *acknowledge him*." The Hebrew says literally, "In all your ways *know* him," which I like better. "Acknowledge" is a weak word, something we do with a nod of the head to someone across the room or when passing out an employee-of-the-month plaque. But we are to "know" God, intimately, with our whole being, along every path at every moment.

That sounds all pious and beautiful when I type it, but I actually can't think of a more threatening idea: don't make a move without complete, trusting surrender to God, rather than relying on our own thinking. The proverb, after all, doesn't say, "Believe in the Lord with all of your heart," but "trust."

*Trust* is an all-in, no-wiggle-room word. It's a hard word.

# There Goes Jesus
# Being Jesus Again

And then there's Jesus. He tells a famous story that turns upside down any distorted thoughts we might have of what it means to "believe" in God.

In the Sermon on the Mount, Jesus tells his audience not to worry and fret about how much they have, what they wear, or what they will eat. That's what people of "little faith" do. Rather, the focus should be on seeking to live in harmony with God's will and to trust God for the rest (Matthew 6:25–34).

I have a love-hate relationship with this story because it both is liberating and also tells me to do something I don't want to do and that I'm not very good at it when I try. A simply delightful nature-nurture trait I picked up from my immigrant parents is a disposition toward anxiety, a preoccupation with all sorts of possible futures. Fretting about the things Jesus says not to fret about is what I do best.* I should

---

* Which reminds me of the famous quote by Mark Twain: "I have lived a long life and had many troubles, most of which never happened."

offer a graduate-level course, and maybe one day I will. It's my safe space, my home field. But Jesus says not to worry about what might happen and instead trust God for now and tomorrow.

Okay. Fine. I'm listening.

Jesus illustrates his point in what is, frankly, a ridiculously off-topic reference to the lilies of the field and the birds of the air: "See, they're doing just fine because God takes care of them. So what are you so worried about?"

Seriously, Jesus? Are you taking questions?

(*I raise my hand. Jesus nods in my direction.*)

ME. *I appreciate the effort, Jesus, but to state the obvious, and I think I speak for everyone here, lilies don't have brains and birds are skittish little things that fly into windows. I, on the other hand, am a human being. I have a brain, not to mention a house and family. I have to pay bills in a crappy economy while trying to keep my kids safe from drugs and predators, let alone getting them into a good college, and somehow paying for it without selling my body parts to science or moving into a storage facility. So forgive my condescending smile when I hear you comparing me and my problems to plants and birds like they're my role models. Birds are birds and plants are plants, Jesus. By definition, they don't have the capacity for thought that even makes worrying possible. By definition, they literally have no worries! They are incapable of worry.*

JESUS. *You're right more than you know. Yes, plants and birds by definition are incapable of worry.*

ME. *Ugh. Are you going to answer my question without really answering it, like you do with those Pharisees or like Yahweh did to Job? Because that gets old and I'm not in the mood.*

JESUS. *I am telling you to consider the lilies of the field and the birds of the air because they are, like you said, by definition, incapable of worry.*

ME. *? . . . ? . . . ?*

JESUS. *If you truly trust the Father, you too will be, by definition, incapable of worry.*

ME. *Uh . . . hmm . . . .*

JESUS. *Worry will be as impossible for you as it is for insentient plants and clueless birds. When you trust, when you let go of your life and lean on God with your whole heart, worry will fade from your vocabulary. You will be as oblivious to the cares of this world as are plants and birds. And then you will be free—free of worry. Get it?*

ME. *So . . . you mean "Don't worry" isn't just a quote for a Bible poster featuring cute animals? You actually mean this?*

JESUS. *What's a Bible poster? And yes.*

Maybe we should train ourselves to use different words to talk about faith. "Believing in God" doesn't get us to that place Jesus describes here. Belief leaves room for worry. Trust explodes it.

I don't mean to sound preachy. I'm far from having that kind of trust. I have trouble trusting my kids to hang the car keys back up so I can find them later, let alone trusting God with my existence. After all, it's my life we're talking about here. Can't I just write books about what I believe *about* God? I'm doing that right now, and I really like it. I spent like most of my twenties and thirties in school working on it. Or can't I just go to church, recite a creed, and talk about what I believe, because, after all . . .

JESUS. *If I may interrupt, no you can't, Peter. No you can't. It doesn't work that way. You have to risk, let go, and trust. Trust me that you'll be better off for it. I won't let you stay in that safe place where you can play with your thoughts and turn them around in your mind. I will make sure that sooner or later all your thoughts and words will make you (not just your family and students) miserable. You must take the harder path, the way of complete trust that you can't pull off without trusting me enough to trust me. And yes, I know that's a paradox. You have to surrender, no matter what you happen to be thinking, no matter what you say you believe at the moment.*

What a way to live. It's like a high-stakes trust fall—and there's a reason they don't call it a "belief fall." We actually have to fall backwards, not cogitate on whether we "believe" the other person will catch us. Even though we are pretty certain we won't crack our head on the floor, we still have to go through with it and risk the possibility, with that sudden rush of fear that comes over us.

Harder still is the Jesus trust fall—because it's not an icebreaker game at a sales convention and we're not always sure he's standing there behind us. In fact, like the psalmists, Qohelet, and Job, some of us might feel as if God has actually let us drop to the floor one too many times. I get that—and maybe that's why we have psalmists telling us they have trouble sleeping at night:

> I am weary with my moaning;
>> every night I flood my bed with tears;
>> I drench my couch with my weeping.
> (Psalm 6:6)

Trusting God isn't just hard. Waking up at 6:00 A.M. to go to work when you've been up half the night with the baby is hard. Working two shifts is hard. Sending your first child off to college is hard. But trusting God is an all-in surrender that covers our egos with a thick tarp. Trusting God is death. And trusting God can be excruciating when we're yet again waiting for God to show up and then doesn't.

As we've seen, some biblical writers were honest about not being able to trust God. They might not even have *wanted* to trust God at the moment. Yet they're still talking to God. They can't let it go. They still *want to* trust God.

Sometimes that's the best we can do. And we're in good company. Thomas Merton's well-known prayer puts it this way:

My Lord God, I have no idea where I am going. I do not see the road ahead of me. I cannot know for certain where it will end. Nor do I really know myself, and the fact that I think that I am following your will does not mean that I am actually doing so. But I believe that the desire to please you does in fact please you. And I hope I have that desire in all that I am doing. I hope that I will never do anything apart from that desire. And I know that if I do this you will lead me by the right road though I may know nothing about it. Therefore will I trust you always though I may seem to be lost and in the shadow of death. I will not fear, for you are ever with me, and you will never leave me to face my perils alone.

Trust is not for the weak. It's the excruciating option, especially if you feel God has let you down. But it's *the* option for the life of faith; there's no getting around it. Trust takes full surrender and courage all at the same time. Another paradox.

One option is definitely not open to us—replacing trust with the safer option, belief, of being left alone with controlling God and turning God about in our heads. The entire idea of true faith seems designed to make sure *that* kind of faith—clinging to certainty in our beliefs—melts away like an ice cube on a red-hot skillet.

If I were king of Christianity, after limiting church services to forty-five minutes and sermons to ten, as well as outlawing church "share time" altogether, I would proclaim a kingdom-wide decree that, at least for a while until we get it, "believe" should be stricken from all of our Bibles and replaced with *trust*.

The content—the *what*—has its place. But if the *who* is not central, if it's not personal, the *what* doesn't count for us, at least not when life turns sour. I believe that God is more interested in the *who*. And that means walking the walk, not just talking the talk.

Better: it means walking the walk when no words are left. *That* is trust.

# But, But . . . What About . . . ?

I imagine some might be thinking of Bible verses that do seem to focus on *believing* and *having faith* as content words, of knowing what you believe, and they might want to know what to do with them.

For example, James writes that those who lack wisdom need only ask for it, but to

> ask in faith, *never doubting,* for the one who doubts is like
> a wave of the sea, driven and tossed by the wind; for the
> doubter, being *double-minded and unstable* in every way, must
> not expect to receive anything from the Lord. (James 1:6–8;
> emphasis added)

It looks like *faith* is an intellectual word because *faith* means "never doubting," and doubters receive nothing from God. So I suppose we'd better be certain about what we believe without a shred of doubt creeping in.

But no. For one thing, if faith means never ever doubting, some psalmists, Qohelet, and Job are in big trouble. They clearly don't do what James says here, but I don't think we want to cancel their voices out as "double-minded and unstable in every way"!

The Bible is a book of diverse voices that speaks into diverse situations and says what needs to be said then and there. One verse doesn't cancel the other out.

We also need to look at the verses above this passage. We see that James is writing to those who are facing personal trials—probably hostility and physical threats because of their faith in Christ. Sometimes in the life of faith we need to hear "God will not abandon you when you are struggling with trusting God." Other times, in the heat of threats that many of us can't relate to (at least I can't), we might need to hear "This, right now, is NOT the time to dwell on your struggles with trusting God, but the time to trust God completely." Persecution tends to simplify our choices.

Still, I often hear that true faith means having steel-hard certainty about the truth of Christianity—not only for our own sake, but to be a good debater, win arguments, and be locked and loaded to defend the faith and convince people that Christianity is the one true religion.

> Always be ready to make your defense to anyone who
> demands from you an accounting for the hope that is in you.
> (1 Peter 3:15)

But here too we need to look at the surrounding verses. Just as with the book of James, 1 Peter was written during a time of persecution. The persecuted readers aren't being told that they need to be intellectually certain of God's existence and communicate effectively to atheists and pagans how they know they're right. Rather, in the face of persecution, Peter wants them to be prepared at any moment to bear witness to the God they *trust with their very lives.*

Peter isn't recommending a tutoring session so they get the right information down. He is encouraging them not to be overcome by fear but to trust God and be able to say so when the executioner is sharpening his ax.

Yes. Always be ready. Cultivate trust so it is strong when you need it.

I've known people suffering from terminal illness who say they've been preparing for this moment their whole lives without knowing it. They've been in all sorts of situations and seasons of life where they needed to let go of control and trust God. And now, facing the biggest letting-go moment, as we all will, their training is paying off. Trusting God has been a habit, which is now ready and able to strengthen them in their hour of need. They are ready to give to those around them "an account of the hope" they have.

Peter isn't giving debate tips. He's talking about trusting God in life and death.

*Belief* and *faith* always have content—a *what.* But a faith that looks like what the Bible describes is rooted deeply in trust in God (rather than ourselves) and in faithfulness to God by being humbly faithful to others (as the Father and Son have been faithful to us). That's basically it—though it's anything but easy.

A life of faith that accepts this biblical challenge is much more demanding than being preoccupied with correct thinking—because that deeper faith is self-denying.

That is the kind of faith we are all called to, and I am glad the Bible models it for us—a faith where our first impulse in the face of life's challenges is to trust God rather than figure out what God is doing so we can get a handle on life.

Ah yes. Life. Ready and waiting to deliver those challenges right to our front door with no warning and when we least expect it.

Life's challenges mock and then destroy a faith that rests on correct thinking and the preoccupation with defending it. And that is a good thing. Life's challenges clear the clutter so we can see more clearly that faith calls for trust instead.

Chapter
Six

# Uh-Oh: When Certainty Is Caught Off Guard (and Why That Might Not Be Such a Bad Idea)

Do not be far from me, for trouble is near and there is
no one to help.

—Psalm 22:11

But sir, if the LORD is with us, why then has all this happened
to us? And where are all his wonderful deeds that our ancestors
recounted to us . . . ?

—Judges 6:13

# When Life Happens

Life happens, and when it does, it wreaks havoc with our neatly arranged thoughts of God, the world, and our place in it. These are moments where deep down something shifts and a quiet voice says, "Uh-oh. I don't like that feeling at all. How can I make it go away?"

These uh-oh moments can happen while watching a Disney movie on a plane; channel surfing and landing on a show where something clicks; reading a novel that challenges our way of looking at the world (and makes more sense). Oh heck, simply being conscious, living and breathing, working, raising a family, having friends, and meeting new people give us ample opportunity to field challenges that come at us from any and all directions.

And each time we do—each time we deal with something outside of our familiar patterns of thought and have to think on our feet and decide how to proceed—our ordered world grounded in a certain faith gets left behind bit by bit until "certainty" becomes past tense.

It seems to me that life is a series of challenges to any notion of faith that is preoccupied with correct thinking. And life can be hard enough without having the added pressure of thinking we need to be able to have it all make sense and fit within the structures of our minds. But a faith that requires us to hold on to what we "know" becomes, we eventually discover, inadequate for handling the peaks and valleys of our humanity. It's also exhausting to try to hold it all together as it once was.

I think there is another way forward, and it is by *listening* to our uh-oh moments. Paradoxically, the challenges of our day-to-day existence are sustained reminders that our life of faith simply must have its center somewhere other than in our ability to hold it together in our minds. Life is a pounding surf that wears away our rock-solid certainty. The surf always wins. Slowly but surely. Eventually. It may be best to ride the waves rather than resist them.

*What are your one or two biggest obstacles to staying Christian? What are those roadblocks you keep running into? What are those issues that won't go away and make you wonder why you keep on believing at all?*

These are questions I asked on a survey I gave on my blog in the summer of 2013. Nothing fancy. I just asked some questions and waited to see what would happen. In the days to come, I was overwhelmed with comments and e-mails from readers, many anonymous, with bracingly honest answers often expressed through the tears of relentless and unnerving personal suffering.

I didn't do a statistical analysis (who has the time, plus I don't know how), but the responses fell into five categories.

1. The Bible portrays *God as violent,* reactive, vengeful, bloodthirsty, immoral, mean, and petty.

2. The *Bible and science collide* on too many things to think that the Bible has anything to say to us today about the big questions of life.

3. In the face of injustice and heinous suffering in the world, *God seems disinterested* or perhaps unable to do anything about it.

4. In our ever-shrinking world, it is very difficult to hold on to any notion that *Christianity is the only path to God.*

5. *Christians treat each other so badly* and in such harmful ways that it calls into question the validity of Christianity—or even whether God exists.

These five categories struck me as exactly right—at least, they match up with my experience. And I'd bet good money they resonate with a lot of us.

All five categories have one big thing in common: "Faith in God no longer *makes sense* to me." Understanding, correct thinking, knowing what you believe—these were once true of their faith, but no longer are. Because life happened.

A faith that promises to provide firm answers and relieve our doubt is a faith that will not hold up to the challenges and tragedies of life. Only deep trust can hold up.

# God Did *What,* Now?

In the Bible, God is often portrayed as approving or commanding physical violence and death as a means of punishing the wicked and disobedient—not as a last resort, but as God's preferred means of conflict resolution. God appears to be cruel, merciless, and reactive, a sovereign we are afraid to cross. More Jess's God than Leslie's in *Bridge to Terabithia.*

For my blog readers, this cringe factor was mentioned as much as any other: "I was always told to read the Bible every day and accept it as God's word. I did that, and now I wish I hadn't."

Why does God's word make it so hard to believe in God? Why was my faith better off before I decided to read through the Bible book by book and find a God who reminds me more of Idi Amin or Chairman Mao than Jesus? And the pressure from Christian peers and leaders to stop "undermining" or "attacking" the Bible by asking questions like this doesn't help ease the problem but only makes it worse.

Readers mentioned the flood and Noah's ark (Genesis 6–9). The Old Testament contains 923 chapters. By the time we get to the sixth one—the *sixth* one, mind you—God's patience has already run out on the world he created, and he apparently can think of no better solution than to drown every creature, except the chosen family of Noah and two of each kind of animal.

This story isn't for kids. When our children were young, we had hanging over our bedroom door a large wooden carved plaque of smiling cartoonish animals meandering onto the ark while a Santa-like Noah looked on, smiling approvingly. The caption read, "God's promises never fail."

That may be, but I'm not sure that captures the gist of the story. How about "God is so angry and so very sorry for creating humans that he drowns all humans (and animals) except for a small fraction of the population"? I'm not sure where that plaque is now, but it's not on our wall.

High on the list of violent acts was God's command that the Israelites enter Canaan and exterminate every last one of the inhabitants of the land—men, women, and children—and take the land for themselves (Deuteronomy 20:10–18). In one of the battle scenes, Joshua (the leader of the Israelites after Moses died) captures and executes five enemy kings and hangs their bodies on trees until evening (Joshua 10:26). In another scene, Israel's army kills the entire male population and all the women who aren't virgins of nearby Midian, keeping the virgins (which included young girls, to be sure) and dividing them among themselves along with the other spoils of war (Numbers 31).

The New Testament doesn't get off the hook. In the last book of the Christian Bible, Revelation, we read of "one like the Son of Man" (Jesus, apparently) on a cloud with a sickle in his hand, ready to cut down the clusters of grapevines of the earth (Revelation 14:14 16). After being cut down, the vines are tossed into the "great wine press of the wrath of God"—a metaphor for divine retribution against the enemies of God (here, the Roman Empire), where blood "flowed from the wine press, as high as a horse's bridle, for a distance of about two hundred miles" (verses 17–20).

All this (and more) raises a perfectly reasonable question: How is any of this different from the many forms of religiously and ideologically motivated slaughters and pillagings that marked the twentieth century, that we see in the news on a regular basis still, and that Christians are quick to condemn? How can Christians condemn brutal tribal warfare today when the Christian God commanded brutal tribal warfare yesterday? What kind of God are we dealing with here?

It's hard to know what the take-home message is for us. The message seems to be that when God gets angry, he kills a lot of people. Just like other ancient tribal overlords or deities we know from the ancient world of the Bible.

Both Jewish and Christian thinkers have pondered how to think through this troubling tendency in the Bible; some approaches are better than others. But I'm simply pointing out that one of the most basic questions we could ask of the Bible, "What is God like?" becomes a serious challenge when we take the time to read the Bible. Uh-oh moments jump off the page like fleas off a bloodhound. And we have a hard time explaining this God to unsympathetic friends—or to ourselves.

Is the faith in God really supposed to be this hard? With a Bible like this, what *are* we supposed to think about God?

Being certain of what you believe and expecting the Bible to provide that information sounds like a spiritual safety net, and many take it on faith that this way of thinking is normal and nonnegotiable for Christians. But what happens when the Bible becomes a source of trouble and doubt instead—not a source of certainty, but a cause for questioning what you had been so certain about?

I've heard it said more than once: the best book to read if you're thinking of becoming an atheist is the Bible. That's a bit extreme as far as I'm concerned, but by portraying God as violent and retributive, the Bible itself, rather than clarifying the matter, raises some self-evident challenges to what we think God is like.

# Our Pale Blue Dot

It's no secret that the Bible and science don't exactly see eye to eye when it comes to explaining how the world and cosmos came to be and why things are the way they are.

Evolutionary biology, genetics, astrophysics, and geology—to name just a few—have explained much of the universe around us through analysis, experimentation, and observation (some of which we glimpsed in chapter 2). These explanations are compelling and universally accepted among people educated in those fields (with occasional pushback on some details from a small minority). But they don't square up with the Bible.

The Bible gives us a different cosmos altogether, some of which is laid out in the very first book and chapter, Genesis 1. We read there of an earth as a flat disk, a few thousand years old, that sits stationary in the cosmos with the heavenly bodies moving around it. A solid dome of some sort arches from one horizon to the other and keeps back the waters of the "deep" that lie above—the waters that represent the threat of chaos to make the Earth uninhabitable. Rain, hail, and thunder are in heavenly storehouses that God may use as reward and punishment for obedience or disobedience (Jeremiah

10:13; Deuteronomy 28:12, 22). All that we see around us—animal, mineral, or vegetable—was created by God as is.

Most Christians I know don't lose sleep over these sorts of things. But they also see a deeper issue, a nagging buzz of discomfort that gets louder the more they think of it—and this has been a big issue for me, too: the immeasurably vast size of the universe. I know I mentioned this before, but it's unsettling enough that I want to mention it again.

Our universe—to be precise, the "known universe"—is about 13.8 billion years old and 546 sextillion (546 plus twenty-one zeros) miles across; traveling at the speed of light (186,282 miles per second), it would take about 93 billion years to go from one end to the other. This universe contains billions of galaxies, with each one containing billions of stars that are millions of light-years apart. Add to all this the notion that about 85 percent of the universe is made up of something called dark matter. We live in a universe that is truly unfathomably large and awe inspiring, to be sure. But the thought of all this makes me freeze in my tracks.

Our cosmos isn't just what we see up there, as it was in antiquity. The writer of Psalm 19 praises God for creation, for he sees God's glory in the heavens: "The heavens! Just . . . wow. Look up there! Isn't God awesome?!" Hooray for him. This may be all fine and good from an ancient Iron Age perspective, where physical reality is restricted to what you see with your eyes. But my "heavens" aren't "up there." There is no "up." The "heavens" surround us and just keep on going—infinitely, for all intents and purposes.

Seventeenth-century philosopher Blaise Pascal wrote: "The eternal silence of the infinite spaces terrifies me." I'm with him. The thought of the "heavens" is numbing, disorienting, and unsettling to me, enough to make me want to sit down and stop thinking about it all—which is what some of my survey takers also pointed out.

The universe is immeasurably large and old, and our speck-of-dust Earth in one solar system on the outskirts of one lonely galaxy seems insignificant on the grand scale science has revealed. Our home planet, as Carl Sagan put it, is a "pale blue dot," precious to us but of incalculable insignificance on the grand cosmic scale.

What kind of God is this? Where *is* this God? Is "where" even a legitimate question? Is God a being, or is it better to say, as some theologians do, "God *is* being"? That strikes me as a promising train of thought, but what then do we do with the biblical God, who is definitely presented as a person-like deity, who sits enthroned in the heavens?

Who or what is this God, exactly? What does the God of the inexplicably infinitely large and infinitesimally small have to do with the God of the Bible, who seems preoccupied with tribal skirmishes, making sure his people don't eat shellfish or pork, and who demands his people maintain a rigorous schedule of sacrifices to him?

The disconnect between our world and the ancient one is indeed vast when we begin talking about God.

But for many of my survey takers, the even more challenging areas of science were branches of anthropology and psychology—fields that speak more to what makes us human. Now, it's getting personal.

Humans have been around for a long time, doing humanlike things—far longer, more widespread, and more complex than the simple stories of Genesis. We have ancient art in the form of cave drawings forty thousand years old. In Göbelki Tepe, Turkey, archaeologists uncovered the oldest known temple. Whoever these people were, they were worshiping some deity or deities about eleven thousand years ago, predating creation in the Bible by five thousand years.

We know of cave paintings in Mongolia that depict wrestling matches from seven thousand years ago, when, according to the first chapter of the Bible, the cosmos was still trapped in a cosmic, primordial, chaotic "deep" (ocean). The Sumerians (in modern-day Iraq) were brewing beer six thousand years ago, around the time when the Bible says God created light. Stonehenge was built five thousand years ago, one thousand years before Abraham, Israel's first ancestor, came on the scene.

How does the God of the biblical story fit into all this? That question challenges modern-day Christians as no generation before.

Neurobiologists are currently mapping the brain and are able to reproduce human emotions in laboratories—including those associated with worshiping God. Are we, then, as "neurotheologians" put it, simply a mass of chemicals and neurons that have evolved over millions upon millions of years of adaptation? Are humans simply an evolved species with particular adaptive functions, like art and abstract reasoning, that Christians have mistakenly been calling "the image of God?"

Medications have been hugely successful in addressing chemical imbalances in our brains, either innate or learned, that have wired us to act and think in certain ways that might have been called "sinful" in times past. I personally know many perfectly down-the-middle-noncontroversial Christians, including pastors and professors, who have been helped by therapists and Lexapro more than prayer, Bible reading, or some forms of Christian, Bible-based counseling (that emphasize sin and the need for repentance).

If healing wounds and helping people live fulfilling and meaningful lives can be addressed through skilled counselors, group support, and medication, what are we to make of the biblical language of sin to explain why we do what we do?

The question many of faith are confronted with today is whether ancient biblical ways of understanding humanity really have all that much to add to the modern discussion. Does Jesus really make a difference, or are we better off with a health plan that covers therapy and prescription medications? These sorts of questions come up in a modern world awash in genuine, documented, therapeutic successes and pharmacological advances.

We have every reason today to think differently about the universe and our place in it. This doesn't disprove God, but it does challenge our thinking. For people of faith, bringing the ancient Bible and our lives together can be stressful and unnerving—which is a problem if faith and correct thinking are deemed inseparable. "What does it mean to be human?" does not have as clear a biblical answer as it once had.

# Falling Branches

Where is God when we're facing the worst life has to offer—when life explodes in front of us? Some in my survey told stories of sense-less, random, heinous, unjust, and cruel suffering and death that would tax to the breaking point anyone's faith in a just, attentive, and loving God we had always believed in—or whether there's a God out there at all.

Twice in the last several years or so that I've lived in the suburbs of Philadelphia, the evening news reported something so bizarre, so flat-out implausible, and so very tragic, that I was left thinking that either God doesn't exist or spends a lot of time napping or is simply distracted.

While jogging along a wooded trail in an area park, a huge branch high above cracked off its massive trunk and landed on the head of a jogger below. She was listening to music on her iPod and was killed instantly. Those jogging further ahead or behind were fine.

This might not make you jump as it did me, but as a writer and professor, supposedly getting paid to have a good handle on God, I was taken by surprise. I felt my intellectual armor disintegrate, like a blowtorch cutting through whipped cream.

Had she just left the house a few moments sooner or later. Had she just kept up a slightly slower or quicker pace. Had traffic to the park been a bit heavier or lighter. But no.

How can anyone recover from this news? I mean, the timing—like it was all carefully orchestrated. "Branch, drop on top of unsuspecting mortal minding her own business on three . . . two . . . one . . . release."

A few years later, in what seemed to me like a twice-told cruel cosmic nightmare, a young mother was taking a walk in a park, not far from where I live, with her two young sons. This time a branch fell and killed one of the boys at the very moment they passed underneath. The mother and the brother, a few steps away, were not touched.

I don't remember more details. I was too busy shutting down my brain so I wouldn't have to process the implications. For an instant, any talk of God coming from my lips seemed absurd, ridiculous, and foolish. A quick Google search of "child killed by falling branch" brings up a disconcerting number of incidents.

What kind of universe is God running, anyway?

No wonder ancient peoples sacrificed to appease their gods. Pantheons made up of gods with humanlike qualities have their downsides (like being distracted all the time by having sex with humans), but they also have a built-in mechanism for handling "acts of God," as our insurance policies put it. If a high wind dropped a tree branch on a loved one, you could always pin it on the kinds of chess games the gods were known to play with human lives. Solution? Offer a sacrifice, make a vow, or appeal to your patron god to protect you. Belief in the gods themselves, however, didn't seem less plausible.

But once you are left with *one* God who is also all knowing and all loving, "Why do senseless and horrible things happen?" is a lot harder to answer. That's the monotheist's dilemma: a schizophrenic God who is all loving and caring one moment and then distant and uncaring the next.

I don't understand how all this works. Does God cause these things or just let them happen? Is God too busy or disinterested? Keeping branches from falling at just the perfect time—neither a second sooner or later—clearly wasn't a priority.

The Bible doesn't help much here because it contains psalms like this one:

> I lift up my eyes to the hills—
>    from where will my help come?
> My help comes from the LORD,
>    who made heaven and earth.
> He will not let your foot be moved;
>    he who keeps you will not slumber.
> He who keeps Israel
>    will neither slumber nor sleep.
> The LORD is your keeper;
>    the LORD is your shade at your right hand.
> The sun shall not strike you by day,
>    nor the moon by night.
> The LORD will keep you from all evil;
>    he will keep your life.
> The LORD will keep
>    your going out and your coming in
>    from this time on and forevermore.
> (Psalm 121)

No need to worry, because God doesn't slumber. He will watch out for you, and neither the sun nor moon will strike you. Good to hear, but how about adding a clause for falling branches? Imagine reading this psalm to the families. I can't. The Bible—our source of knowing what God is up to—has lost its credibility for some.

I cannot speak to how the surviving family members processed this pain. And I have no right to try. But for me, these episodes pushed me to think differently about God. What I thought I knew about how God works—even if there's a Bible passage to back it up—seemed like a naïve wish, a hypothesis with no support. If there is a God, this God doesn't behave the way I expected.

The faith of some is untouched by all this. But for those who find themselves in a place where the absurdity of God's absence is more real than the touch of their own skin, these uh-oh moments make it hard to force a holy smile and keep on keeping on as before.

The falling branches in our lives force open the doors of our minds to dark and out-of-our-control places with questions that challenge the very core of what we thought we knew about God—and we ask deep down in our guts how knowing what we believe and our absurd reality come together. Once that door is opened, it can't easily be forced closed again. The life of faith is never the same.

We sometimes refer to these perplexities as "mysteries" of God. Yes indeed, mystery—but these mysteries are painful for us to experience, even terrifying and unsettling.

"Mystery" is not a loophole in our defense case for God, certain that the answer is secure and waiting for us behind the curtain. I'm working this out like everyone else, but it seems to me that the way forward is not to "find the answer" that will allow familiar ways of thinking of God and our world to somehow stay as they were. The way forward is to let go of that need to find the answers we crave and decide to continue along a path of faith *anyway* (as Qohelet would say). That kind of faith is not a crutch, but radical trust.

Beyond that, I don't have much to add, except perhaps to point humbly to one of the key pillars (and mysteries!) of the Christian faith, that God enters into human suffering and dies. I'll just leave it at that. If I say more, I'm afraid it will look like I'm trying to explain it.

I am amazed and encouraged by those who have lived through these moments of hell on earth and have continued on in the life of faith anyway. They have something to teach people like me: no matter what we think we know, no matter how sure we happen to think we are, suffering is the place where our sense of certainty about God's ways fades like a dream and forces us to consider that what we know may not be as central to our faith as we might think.

# Meeting New People

Sometimes the biggest challenge to our sense of certainty about God is just getting out of the house once in a while and seeing that we are just people like everyone else with a limited perspective and not the center of the universe. And when we leave our village and interact with real live flesh-and-blood people who see the divine and the world differently, we cannot help but be affected somehow—and perhaps threatened.

*Is what we believe the only way? Are we right and is everyone else wrong?*

*Do I believe as I do simply because of where and when I happened to be born? Would I be a committed Hindu or Buddhist, just as certain about the truth of what I believe, if I were born elsewhere?*

*Can we really say with credibility and a straight face that Christianity—let alone my version of it—has a monopoly on truth?*

Our world has grown very small though technology. We "travel" daily via the Internet, and our familiar world is relativized. Us-versus-them thinking seems absurd. Holding on to correct thinking about God and the world becomes stressful.

When I left my conservative seminary for doctoral work in Old

Testament at Harvard University, one of my professors (who had made a similar journey) said, "The non-Christians there will be some of the nicest people you'll ever meet." Boy, was he right. My most spiritually challenging experience at Harvard wasn't professors who were geared up to strong-arm me into atheism or some Ivy League cult (as some warned). It was, unexpectedly, the simple act of living and working with people outside of my familiar tribe.

My classmates and professors came from such different walks of life, from different countries, and they believed such different things than I—about Jesus, God, the Bible, and the world around us. Many of these good people had no idea, no mental architecture, for how I processed reality through my version of the Christian faith, which I took for granted, assumed to be correct, and never really had to seriously examine before. As I rode the subway, navigated Harvard Square, and walked across Harvard Yard, that sense was multiplied many times over. So many people. So different from me.

And yet, as it turned out, so much the same.

There were no enemies waiting to trip me up, no muggers lurking in the shadows, no snipers on the rooftop. They were the same mixed bag of personalities I've always known, in and out of church, with hopes, fears, histories, and wounds. I shared meals with them and they babysat our children. They were fellow humans, not the "other"—at least no more the "other" than I was to them.

It could have been me. Like them, I could have grown up somewhere else. And if I had, I wouldn't be the person I am now—with my particular set of beliefs ordered and arranged as they are. I could have been a "them."

I wasn't exactly sheltered as a child, but at Harvard, in my late twenties, the time was apparently right for me to begin coming face-to-face with what one might call the randomness of my existence and the inadequacy of my faith structure to account for it. And these people, these "outsiders" whom I was taught would on God's judgment day be consigned to endless punishment, were basically good and kind people—more pleasant, unfortunately, than some Christians I've come across.

So how am I, with my random existence, suddenly the standard by which to evaluate others on earth? Does *God* look on them as outsiders? Are they destined for eternal separation from God because of when and where they were born and raised, while I, being on God's party list, can make it past the bouncer because of when and where I was born and raised?

"Know what you believe" *needs* a "them" as a contrast. But travel broadens. When the bigger world is tossed in our lap, that sort of confidence wanes and the "them" category shrinks. We begin to wonder whether there even is a "them." And we hope that God really does love the world enough to let nothing get in the way—especially where and when someone was born.

More than anything, studying the Bible with Jews dislodged my parochial thinking about God, and it's had a lasting impact. Over time, I came to appreciate firsthand the richness and depth of that tradition. I also felt some shame for never really being exposed to it before, even in seminary.

Early in my first year I had lunch with a Jewish classmate who grew up in Israel. For some reason I can't recall, the topic turned to the story of Adam and Eve (Genesis 2–3). Maybe I was munching on an apple.

The Christian version of this story—the only version I had ever heard—goes like this. Adam and Eve take a bite of the forbidden fruit after being tempted by Satan (here portrayed as a serpent). As a result, God becomes angry with them and throws them out of paradise. Not only so, but this "original sin" caused *all* humanity to "fall" into this same state of being objects of God's complete displeasure. Not a single neuron or hair follicle can escape this state of sin we are all born into, which is the ultimate cause of every conceivable ill on Earth, from tyranny to taxes to charging $2,500 for box seats at Yankee Stadium.

So over lunch, I mentioned casually this fall of humanity.

"The *what*?"

"The fall of humanity. [Duh.] You know, Adam and Eve's disobedience plunged all subsequent humanity into a state of sinfulness and complete alienation from God."

"Never heard of it."

"Really? That's odd, since it's so obvious."

"No, it's not. The story nowhere says anything about sinfulness passed down from parent to child. Death and hardship are introduced to humanity, but nowhere do we read that sinfulness is 'passed down.'"

"Well . . . then what do you make of Satan tempting Eve with the forbidden fruit?"

"Who?"

"What do you mean 'who?'"

"Satan isn't in the story. We see a serpent, and he is clearly identified as the craftiest *creature* made by God—not a supernatural foe of some sort. "

"But the serpent is *talking*."

"Because it's a story."

"Okay, well . . . then tell me why we do bad things?"

"Good question—but one the story of Adam and Eve doesn't answer. Jews believe that humans struggle with an 'evil inclination,' meaning humans are disposed toward sin, which is an idea we *do* find elsewhere in Genesis, in the Flood story: 'The LORD saw that the wickedness of humankind was great in the earth, and that every *inclination* of the thoughts of their hearts was only *evil* continually' (Genesis 6:5; emphasis added). Adam and Eve had that same evil inclination, which explains why they disobeyed."

"Oh. Okay, then."

What I "knew" the story of Adam and Eve to be about wasn't what the story actually said, but something I had brought to the story from my own Christian tradition. How could I have missed it? It was so obvious. I don't mind saying that I felt somewhat duped. And that's a lot to work through over lunch.

My faith and the Bible it was supposedly based on looked awfully fragile. I didn't feel like my faith was being attacked, but relativized—which felt worse.

And that got me thinking: I wonder how much else I was certain about might turn out to be less certain? How naïve and sheltered had I been to think that how I saw things was how they are? And why was I never told any of this? What were they protecting?

All it took to rock my certainty was a conversation over lunch.

I don't claim to have the answers for many of the things that challenge my faith, but this I do believe: I see these moments are invitations to leave my comfort zone and trust God from a place of childlike vulnerability, rather than from a position of power and authority.

And yes, that can be unsettling, unnerving, and even frightening. Leaving home usually is, but I don't think that trust in God is cultivated unless we do.

# When Christians Eat Their Own

A preoccupation with correct thinking isn't just a problem for one's own faith. It can and does have disastrous spiritual consequences for others.

Many in my survey told stories of being badgered, beaten down, betrayed, and bulldozed over the edge by fellow Christians and Christian leaders. And so they stopped going to church, walked away from institutional Christianity in any form, took a long break from God, or simply walked away from the faith altogether.

You can only be misled, mistreated, emotionally abused, manipulated, looked down upon, or lied to by religious leaders and other "brothers and sisters" for so long before packing it in and joining the Rotary Club.

Why did this happen? Because they questioned what they were told to believe. When knowing what you believe is the nonnegotiable center of true faith, questions and critical self-examination pose a threat. It didn't matter how gently and slowly they started conversations. All that mattered was that "the system" was under attack and measures had to be taken.

I'm not talking about simply having disagreements or even arguments where things get out of hand and everyone feels bad later on. That happens, and people of goodwill eventually admit their faults, group hug, and move on.

I'm talking about plain old nastiness as a game plan, a strategy, a badge of honor, evidence of strong faith that protects certainty at all costs and takes no prisoners.

For many in my survey, this was their biggest uh-oh moment to question what they believed. The other four uh-oh moments from the survey called into question the intellectual certainty of their faith—whether it makes sense. But this one involved relationships and communities that let them down, which undermined their faith on a deeper—and for some irreparable—level.

When Christians feel crushed by such "people of God," faith is exposed as something that just doesn't work here and now. And if something doesn't work, intellectual arguments for staying in the faith lose their appeal over time. Why bother?

A faith that eats its own not only drives people out but also sends up a red flare to the rest of humanity that Christianity is just another exclusive members-only club, and that Jesus is a lingering relic of antiquity, rather than a powerful, present-defining spiritual reality; a means of gaining power rather than relinquishing it. And who needs that, really?

Some readers relayed stories that have become all too familiar—caught in the sharp-cutting machinery of church and institutional politics. The dark underbelly of Christian organizations can look more like the dirty political scheming of Francis and Claire Underwood* than the Sermon on the Mount.

---

* From Netflix's smash hit *House of Cards*, a wonderful introduction to notorious Christian politics cleverly masked as a political drama.

Under the high-lofted banner of "defending the gospel," backroom politicking, gossip, maligning the character of their enemies, lying, vengeance, and even destroying people's livelihoods are excused as regrettable yet necessary tactics in their holy war (battle metaphors abound) to root out traitors harboring unbelief. And such causalities, unfortunate as they are, are nevertheless deemed necessary when truth is compromised and the gospel is at stake.

But it seems for some the gospel is always at stake. They have mistaken their own thinking about God with the real thing. They have become so enamored of their own self-referential God talk and believe their own propaganda that they can't tell the difference.

Of course, all organizations, Christian or not, have lines that define who they are. Having boundaries is not the problem. The problem comes when Christians in positions of authority and power (or those seeking to gain it) become tyrannical, strangers to reason, and mow down the opposition all in service of God and God's kingdom. I have heard with my own ears such sub-Christian behavior defended as "just business, nothing personal." You might recognize these words from *The Godfather* movies. This is what is said to someone who is about to get a bullet to the back of the head.

The difference between this uh-oh moment and the other four is glaringly obvious: this one is completely in our control. We can't make Bible difficulties, the modern world, pain and suffering, or contact with other religions go away. But we can stop being mean and ugly. Anytime we want to. If we want to.

And we need to. Jesus says so. And the gospel really *is* at stake. People's lives are at stake.

Preoccupation with correct thinking and holding on with zeal makes us horrible people and those around us miserable. But even here, these can be God moments if we have ears to hear.

Perhaps even here God is present, opening up pathways to other communities of faith for us, to a new way of being Christian, where holding on for dear life to what we "know" isn't front and center. I've found that we can be tied hard and fast even to abusive religious homes, and we don't leave until things get so bad we simply can't stay. Like an abused woman who stays with her abuser because she can't conceive of being anywhere else—until that last time he comes home drunk and violent, and it becomes a matter of survival.

There's nothing like being subject to Christians of ill will to expose the dark underbelly of where the preoccupation with correct thinking can get you—and to begin seeing the value of a different kind of faith. Rather than being the end of faith, these moments can introduce us to a faith rooted in trust rather than certainty.

# God Is Not My Father

Here's a story about a time I knew I was absolutely right and therefore simply knew I was God's appointed mouthpiece at the moment—but God closed my mouth because I was about to say something arrogant and harmful.

I was a new doctoral student in the photocopying room at Harvard Divinity School. The room was a snug fit back in those days, with barely enough room to fit two photocopiers and two high-energy students who each needed to make photocopies for that thing they're working on that would, given time, likely change all human knowledge—or even better, actually land them a tenure-track job. (Cue the sound of God laughing.)

I entered with my load of very heavy and serious books and journals to find someone already furiously at work—a mere underling master's student, and so I doubted very much what she was working on was nearly as important as my world-changing project, the topic of which I can't quite seem to recall at the moment.

She gave me a quick "you're invading my space, get out" glance before refocusing on her work—like a lioness shielding her kill from a pack of hyenas, which, sadly, is par for the course in academia ("*My* knowledge! Keep away!").

Seeing that we were the only two around, and as I always thought of myself as a friendly chap, I thought I'd break the ice.

"Hi, I'm Pete. What are you working on?"

She turned slowly, like in those movies where the totally calm but crazy killer—who is in no hurry because she knows she's in complete control and she's going to kill you either now or later, it doesn't matter to her one way or another—turns around slowly to face the camera and by the time you see her eyes you know it's too late.

With her hellish red squinting eyes aimed right at me—a cross between annoyance and rage—she spoke through teeth grit so tight she might have started a fire in her mouth.

"I'm . . . writing . . . a paper . . . on why . . . God . . . shouldn't be . . . thought of . . . as . . . father."

And with that, here's how God showed up that day.

It might help to know that at this point in my life as a Christian in my late twenties I was somewhere between a pretty nice guy and an arrogant know-it-all. It just depended on the day. On this particular day, my reflex was to ask to her, kindly, without the slightest hint of condescension, and bathed in the light of Christ, how she could be so stupid.

Hadn't she ever actually *read* the Bible? God is male and one of the things this male God is called is "Father." Look it up. Deal with it. The most famous prayer in the world (for heaven's sake), the Lord's Prayer, that one we say in church every Sunday (you *do* go to church, don't you?), the prayer Jesus taught his disciples, starts "Our Father"—not just "my" but "our." We *get* to call God "Father," and Jesus said so.

So back off, photocopying master's student who doesn't know her Bible, doesn't really take Jesus seriously, or doesn't believe in God. Kindly stop annoying the rest of us by making God conform to your half-baked ideas and don't dignify your "theory" by writing a paper about it. I mean, seriously.

"God shouldn't be thought of as father." Those words were like the Bat-signal, and I was there to save the day. But I will make this as painless as possible. I am merciful. She'll never know what hit her.

In a flash, this is what was going on inside my head.

But I didn't say any of that. All that came out of my mouth was, "Wow, that's really interesting." Some crime-fighter I turned out to be.

I turned back around and kept copying. I felt a bit guilty for not having the guts to accept this golden opportunity, orchestrated by God directly, no doubt—for this misguided, clearly wrong, utterly lost master's student to meet God. And I blew it.

But in time I came to see that I hadn't blown it. God had actually kept me from blowing it by stepping in and gagging me.

*You know, Pete (I talk to myself a lot), maybe . . . maybe . . . you need to listen more than talk. Maybe that student has a story to tell. Maybe she has had a rough life, a bad father.*

*Maybe she was sexually abused.*

*Maybe thinking of God as father brings up all sorts of memories and pain. You saw how angry she got!*

*Maybe my little "defending God" speech that I was so sure about would have done more harm to this person that my theology also tells me is made in God's image and therefore precious and of inestimable worth.*

*(I'm not finished. Come back here.) And rather than thinking you are right about God just because you've convinced yourself that you are, maybe you don't have a handle on God like you think you do and you*

*have a few things to learn—like the parts where God actually does love the world and has nurturing patience like a mother and isn't sitting around to use you to squash others.*

This wasn't my only moment of awakening, but I remember this one clearly, perhaps because it happened early on in my life at Harvard. And like other big moments in life, it took me by surprise while I was just going about my business on autopilot.

I believe God mercifully gave me a moment of clarity. Looking back, I see there is much more I could have said to express God's love to this student. But at least I didn't do any harm. I'll take it. Along the way I came to see more and more that being right about God and making sure everyone else agreed with what I knew might not be the most important thing I could do in God's eyes.

In fact—and here is the real mind bender for a seminary graduate/doctoral student in Bible—maybe I'm not even as right about God as my trickster brain wants me to think. Maybe loving other people, which in this case was simply keeping my trap shut, saying a kind word, and not taking the anger personally, was the truly right thing to do.

Maybe my purpose on earth isn't to be the thought police first and love others after all their ideas line up as they should. Maybe my first order of business is to risk my own sense of certainty about God and love others where and how they are no matter how they do on my theology exam.

It's much easier acting on the need to be right than letting go of that need and risking what we hold dear and loving others without expecting anything back or thinking we are scoring points with God. Love happens whether we feel it or not. Love is an action, a selfless act, something we do for others without thinking of ourselves or how it will make us look. Loving others is the most self-emptying, self-denying, thing we can do, because true love has the other person on the top shelf.

As Jesus told a listening crowd long ago, when you love others you are acting most like God at that very moment (Matthew 5:43–48).

The crowd that Jesus addressed was in some ways no different than one would be in our day. Their impulse, as is ours, was to love their neighbor—those most like them—and to hate their enemies—which in Jesus's day most likely referred to the Romans, who did not share much of anything with the Jews, least of all religious beliefs.

But Jesus stared right into this "us vs. them" mindset and told the crowd that they should love their enemies, too. In fact, they should pray for them, even when those enemies were persecuting them (which happened now and then with the Roman government in charge).

When "us vs. them" is your way of life, loving a "them" is hard enough. Praying for a "them" is harder still. We want to pray down God's blood-curdling war cry of wrath and pestilence—or at least pierce and wound them with our sharp words while making photocopies. But Jesus says *enough of that*. To be like God means to be perfect in love (verse 48). To love as God loves means loving not just others like us, but those who are not. And in my case that meant simply keeping my mouth shut when every part of me wanted to speak.

Two thousand years after Jesus spoke these words, the "us vs. them" mindset is still quite common among Christians. It takes hard work and vigilance to see how we can put Jesus's words into practice in different ways and places. That's what Christians do: we read the

Bible, written at a different time for reasons that were relevant back then, and ask ourselves, "What does it look like for us to follow Jesus like that right here and right now?"

At that moment, love meant letting go of something dear to me—being right and winning an argument—even though my brain, like an unruly preschooler, was jumping up and down demanding to be heard.

We're not always too happy about letting go of our egos and telling our overactive thought world to take a seat over there and be quiet. "Knowing" has been in charge for so long, we forget all the other stuff we read in the Bible about how we are to act toward each other.

And here is the risk of love. When we love as Jesus describes, *we* are changed because we are letting go a little bit of what we were holding to so dearly—in my case, being right and saying so. We relax our grip, step out of ourselves, and truly see things from the perspective of someone else, which is a genuinely selfless act.

But change is hard. We often prefer forcing change on others rather than looking at ourselves—seeing the speck in our neighbor's eye rather than the log in our own (Matthew 7:1–5). That's not love.

I still think and talk about what I think God is like, but I've hopefully learned (feel free to keep me honest here, people) that being right and winning isn't the endgame here. Loving as God loves is.

# When "Uh-Oh" Becomes "Ah-Ha"

I probably don't need to say it at this point, but just in case I do: I'm not the answer man. If I had suggested that there were straightforward answers to these uh-oh moments, I'd simply be replacing one kind of certainty for another. I don't think we can solve these problems and get back to a time when everything made sense. I want to see where these problems can lead, to someplace we might never have thought to look had we stayed where we were.

Though for some, that ship has already sailed—like for many of those who answered my survey.

So without wanting this to sound like a ten-point plan for success in life (especially since I only have seven points), I'd like to lay out briefly how I have reimagined thinking about God and faith in God. Not "Do this and that," but "Here's how I am currently seeing the landscape upon which I work out my story of faith, reoriented around trust in God rather than needing to be certain about God." And all of these come out of the kinds of uh-oh moments we just looked at, and some others I want to come back to a bit later on.

1. *Thank you, modernity.* As we've seen, the last few centuries of at least the Western and westernized world have certainly posed scientific challenges to the Christian faith. But as I see it, these challenges have really exposed the problems of a certain kind of faith, one that has fused together correct thinking and strong faith.

The challenges of modernity have shaken our sense of certainty and, in doing so, pushed us toward trust.

Since our children were very young, we have made the family trek each year to a tree farm to cut down our own tree, thereby stepping into a Norman Rockwell painting and an old-fashioned Christmas. After we (by which I mean I) cut it down, we (I) drag the tree over and place it in a tree shaker, a high-speed vibrating stand that shakes out the dead needles and, as the tree guy told me just last year, to get rid of any varmints that might be living in there.

If the tree stayed in the shaker the entire season, it wouldn't be of use to anyone. But it's needed to get the tree to what it can become: a symbol of joy, peace, and celebration.

The modern world has shaken our thinking about God—and maybe that needed to happen.

2. *We can't get our minds around God.* I don't think the Christian faith is fundamentally rational, by which I mean it cannot be captured fully by our rational faculties—and in fact, more often than not, confounds them. A God who can be comfortably captured in our minds, with little else for us to find out apart from an occasional adjustment, is no God at all. Expecting faith in God to be rational is often more the problem than the solution.

As I've said before, I am not for one minute saying reason doesn't matter. I am reasoning as I write this. I mean only that the life of the mind has its place as *an aspect* of the life of faith because it is a dimension of our humanity, and neither the gatekeeper nor the whole.

In other words, I believe that faith in the Creator is necessarily transrational (not antirational) and mystical. I try to remember that as I work through intellectual challenges—and I mean *work through*, not avoid.

3. *Christianity is a setup for letting go of certainty.* The two pillars of the Christian faith express the mystery of faith: incarnation and resurrection. Of course, there's more to the Christian faith, but two elements make Christianity what it is, and both dodge our powers of thought and speech.

Incarnation. God becomes one of us. What does that mean, really? What words are we to use to express it, let alone comprehend it?

Resurrection. The grand reversal of the only true inevitability of all who have ever lived—death.

Both are utterly beyond what is knowable by most every standard we use to know everything else: experience, observation, and testing. These mysteries are "known" differently—only by trust.

I don't mind saying I find it strangely comforting that walking the path of Christian faith means being confronted moment by moment with what is counterintuitive and ultimately beyond my comprehension to understand or articulate. In an unexpected way, God becomes more real to me, not less.

4. *Adjusting our expectations about what the Bible can deliver.* This has been huge for me, since I "do Bible" for a living and I can't get away from thinking about it.

I've learned to accept this paradox: a holy book that more often than not doesn't act very much like you'd expect it, but more like a book written two thousand to three thousand years ago would act.

I expect the Bible to reflect fully the ancient settings in which it was written, and therefore not act as a script that can simply be dropped into our lives without a lot of thought and wisdom. The Bible must be thought through, pondered, tried out, assessed, and (if need be) argued with—all of which is an expression of faith, not evidence to the contrary.

5. *God-moments.* I have had a few God moments in my life. I'd like to have more, but maybe I'm just not paying attention.

Trust your experiences, your God moments. They don't work as intellectual arguments for God, but that's exactly the point: intellectual arguments aren't enough, and wanting them to be so sooner or later leads to disappointment. God speaks to us through our whole humanity, not just through part of it.

God moments can't be proven to anyone else, but that doesn't make them second best. They are proof—of another kind.

6. *God is not a crutch.* As a brain-oriented person, I have tended in my life to look down on those who say things like "If I didn't have my faith, I couldn't make it through this," or "If God isn't real, I don't know if I can hold it together." These sorts of sentiments always struck me as for the weak-minded, those who needed a crutch. If Christianity is true, it has to be for reasons other than "I need it to be true."

I'm older now and have left some of my stupidity behind. I see now, as many others have, that those who cry out to God may be perched at the very point where true communion with God begins, because they are in the unique position of surrendering fully from self to God.

7. *Struggling with faith is normal. Journey* and *pilgrimage* have become powerful words for me for describing the life of faith.

I have come to expect periods of unsettledness, uncertainty, and fear to remind me that who I am, where I am, and what I think do not define reality. Facing and then truly being present with my experiences along the way help me remember that my experiences at any moment are not the entire journey—including those periods where God is distant.

I have come to believe that periods of struggling and doubt are such common experiences of faith, including in the Bible, that something is meant to be learned from such periods, however long in duration they might be.

I feel it is part of the mystery of faith that things normally do not line up entirely, and so when they don't, it is not a signal to me that the journey is at an end but that I am still on it.

As I reflect on my own experience and that of many others far wiser than I, God seems willing to help that process along.

# God Wants You Dead

You have put me in the depths of the Pit, in the regions
dark and deep.

—Psalm 88:6

# The Lie: "It's All Your Fault"

Doubt—not fashionable skepticism, but *really* doubting what you were always so certain of. Many of us—maybe most of us—get there sooner or later.

Perhaps it was a big catastrophe or (and I think more commonly) a line of smaller things that creep in over time, complicate faith, and make us a lot less certain than we used to be.

But whatever the reason(s), when we feel that moment coming on, what do we do? We try to push that feeling down, hoping it will eventually go away before God notices.

It doesn't and God does.

Feeling our familiar faith unravel is unsettling, disorienting, exhausting, and even frightening.

*Where did all this come from, and how can I get back to normal?*
*There must be something very wrong with me.*
*Maybe I'm not smart enough.*
*Maybe I'm a faker and finally being found out.*
*Maybe I haven't memorized enough Bible verses.*
*Maybe I need to go to church more often.*

Whatever the reason, our reflex is to assume we are doing something wrong: "It's all my fault. God must be so disappointed in me. I'm so weak."

So we do the only thing we know how to do, what we've been conditioned to do. We roll up our sleeves and do everything in our power to get out of that state of uncertainty and back to a normal state of rock-solid certainty as quickly as we can; our faith is broken, and it needs to be fixed. Then, when we have our act together and feel we can face God again without shame, we'll jump back into the way things were before, how they're supposed to be.

If none of that works, if doubt holds on too long, here are our choices: live a life of quiet and wretched desperation, shamed or afraid to speak up, or cash in our God chips, press factory reset, and move on.

But doubt is not the enemy of faith, a solely destructive force that rips us away from God, a dark cloud that blocks the bright warm sun of faith. Doubt is only the enemy of faith when we equate faith with certainty in our thinking.

Doubt is what being cornered by our thinking looks like. Doubt happens when needing to be certain has run its course.

Doubt can certainly leave us empty and frightened, but that is precisely the benefit of doubt: it exposes the folly that strong faith means you need to "know what you believe," that the more faith you "have," the more certain you are.

Doubt means spiritual relocation is happening. It's God's way of saying, "Time to move on."

Doubt is powerful. It can do things spiritually that must be done that we would never do on our own. Doubt has a way of forcing our hand and confronting us with the challenge of deeper trust in God, rather than leaning on the ideas we have been holding in our minds about God. Doubt exposes our frail thinking.

We might be accustomed to thinking of our faith as a castle—where we go to be safe and protected. That's a good place to be, and we all need that experience now and then. But what if God isn't a helicopter parent? What if feeling safe and secure isn't always a sign of God's presence but a pattern of fear that keeps God at a distance? And what if God wants to close that gap, for our sake, and doubt helps get us there? Doubt isn't a sign of spiritual weakness but the first steps toward a deeper faith.

Doubt tears down the castle walls we have built, with the false security and permanence they give, and forces us outside to walk a lonely, trying, yet cleansing road. In those times, it definitely feels like God is against us, far away, or absent altogether. But what if the darkness is actually a moment of God's presence that *seems* like absence, a gift of God to help us grow up out of our little ideas of God?

Doubting God is painful and frightening because we think we are leaving God behind, when in fact we are only leaving behind ideas about God that we are used to surrounding ourselves with—the small God, the God within our control, the God who moves in our circles, the God who agrees with us.

Doubt strips away distraction so we can see more clearly the inadequacies of who we think God is and move us from the foolishness of thinking that *our* god is *the* God.

Many of us, I would imagine, think we have God figured out pretty well—and for people like me, who get paid to tell people what God is like, it's an occupational hazard. We read the Bible and are able to quote it to others. We go to church like clockwork and get involved in groups and service projects. We're doing great, and God must surely be impressed.

It is so easy to slip into "right thinking" mode—that we have arrived at full faith. We know what church God goes to, what Bible translation God prefers, how God votes, what movies God watches, and what books God reads. We know the kinds of people God approves of. God has winners and losers, and we are the winners, the true insiders. God likes all the things we like. We speak for God and think nothing of it.

All Christians I've ever met who take their faith seriously sooner or later get caught up in thinking that God really is what we think God is, that there is little more worth learning about the Creator of the cosmos. God becomes the face in the mirror.

By his mercy, God doesn't leave us there.

# The Truth: "God Wants You Dead"

Doubt signals not God's death but the need for our own—to die to the theology we hold to with clenched fists. Our first creeping feelings of doubt are like the distant toll of a graveyard chapel, alerting us that the dying process is coming our way.

God wants us dead. Or better: God wants us to get used to the need to die, not once, but as a pattern for our lives.

In Matthew's Gospel, Jesus tells his followers to take up their crosses and lose their lives so they can find them.

> Whoever loves father or mother more than me is not worthy of me; and whoever loves son or daughter more than me is not worthy of me; and whoever does not take up the cross and follow me is not worthy of me. Those who find their life will lose it, and those who lose their life for my sake will find it. (Matthew 10:37–39)

Jesus isn't antifamily, telling his audience to blow off mom, dad, or the kids and spend all their time walking two steps behind Jesus. Jesus is making an in-your-face point, as he often does.

At the end of the day, what is (or should be) most dear to us? When our light begins to fade and when we come to the end of our lives, what is most likely to be on our minds? Family, those on Earth we are connected to more closely than anyone; when they suffer, we suffer; when they die, we are torn apart; when they triumph, we rejoice.

Following Jesus doesn't mean making a decision to literally hate our families. He means that following him requires an overhaul of our most basic, otherwise-unquestioned, top priorities—those things we cling to, including our thinking. Pitting family against the kingdom of God gets across how drastic and unsettling that overhaul is.

As does "If any want to become my followers, let them deny themselves and take up their cross daily and follow me." A cross is certainly a heavy piece of wood, and most people have seen enough Jesus movies with him beaten, sweaty, and bloodied, struggling to carry his cross through the streets and up to Golgotha to be crucified.

Crosses are heavy, yes, but that's not the point. You don't take up a cross simply to carry it. You take up your cross to die on it. That's the point of crosses.

Following Jesus isn't like a burden we carry on our shoulders. It's an internal process so radical and painful that the best way to describe it for people of that day is as the act of being bound and nailed like a criminal to a piece of wood lifted above the ground where you are left hanging in naked humiliation and intense pain until you suffocate.

And that's a far cry from the claim of some televangelists that "Jesus wants to make you rich and successful." Jesus wants to make us whole. That requires a process up for the challenge.

Physical death is the final letting go that we all experience with loved ones and that we will ourselves experience one day. Dying now the way Jesus says to means letting go already of every comfort, familiarity, joy, and sorrow—and of the false sense of control those things give us. Letting go of these things is a dying process.

Jesus sounds more like a mystic than an intellectual lining up correct thinking.

We have to die, and the choice is ours. If we don't, we are still holding on to something. And if we are holding on, we aren't really following. Just sort of following. Standing around.

*[Oh God, what did I sign up for? This Christianity thing is hard. Deep breath . . .]*

The apostle Paul chimes in, too:

I have been crucified with Christ; and it is no longer I who live, but it is Christ who lives in me. (Galatians 2:19–20)*

The life of Christian faith is more than agreeing with a set of beliefs about Christ, morality, or how to read the Bible. It means being so intimately connected to Christ that his crucifixion is ours, his death is our death, and his life is our life—which is hardly something we can grasp with our minds. It has to be experienced. It *is* an experience.

We're so crucified, in fact, that we read elsewhere, "You have died, and your life is hidden with Christ in God" (Colossians 3:3). Our lives are hidden—strong language, like we're not even in the picture.

---

* English translations of this passage tend to be too wordy and smooth over Paul's rugged and urgent prose. A better rendering is, "I have been crucified with Christ. I no longer live; Christ lives in me."

And being hidden with Christ and being "in" God sounds downright mystical enough to unsettle—as it should—anyone who thinks that the Christian's first duty is to make sure to think the right thoughts.

And all this talk of dying and being crucified and hidden doesn't describe a one-time moment of conversion when we "become Christians," as if that's final. If things were only that easy—a one-time transaction of "accepting Jesus" and then it's over. Dying describes a mode of existence we agree to once we enter the holy space of being a follower of Jesus—surrendering control, dying, all the time.

*[Oh God, this is so much easier to write about than to do. Keep writing . . . keep writing . . .]*

Dying is the normal mode of Christian existence, a pattern of life, what followers of Jesus are to do not just once but every day, every moment. It is certainly not a problem to be fixed so we can return to "normal," as we were.

The choice is always and ever before us: whether we will hold on right here and now to what is dear, to what we know, to the familiar and safe, to twist and bend all of our experiences of God into our own shape, to paint God's image according to our own blurred and sorry self-portraits—or whether we let go of frantic thoughts, die to ourselves, and let God bring us back to life in God's way and time.

That's what Paul is after. Dying leads to real living—"Christ who lives in me," a life so deeply connected to the divine that we no longer live, but our lives are "hidden with Christ in God."

Dying "with" Jesus leads to new life now, what Paul calls a movement "from death to life" (Romans 6:1–14). This is good news, the best news. When we "die," God doesn't leave us dead. God brings us back to life—"raising us from the dead," as Paul puts it. We die in order to be raised, and not just in a future one-day-at-the-end-of-the-world way we talk about at funerals. Dying and rising is how followers of Jesus live and experience God in the present.

Being "saved" by God is an ongoing process of growth and transformation, of dying and rising, of being "conformed to the image of his [God's] Son," as Paul puts it (Romans 8:29). Following Jesus means experiencing the taste of resurrection and ascension now—whether doing laundry, paying bills, or leading nations.

Getting there is all about dying, and each cycle of dying and rising we come to in our lives brings us, I believe, to greater insight into our deep selves, where Christ lives "in us" and our lives are "hidden" in God.

Of course, we all know that dying, rising again, Christ in me, hidden in God, seated in heaven are metaphors—the use of common language to grasp the uncommon, a reality too deep and thick for conventional vocabulary. Following Jesus is an inside-out transformation so thorough that dying and coming back to life is the only adequate way to put it.

Doubt signals that this process of dying and rising is underway. Though God feels far away, at that moment God may be closer than we realize—especially if "know what you believe" is how we're used to thinking of our faith.

Doubt isn't cool, hipster, or chic. Doubt isn't a new source of pride. Don't go looking for doubt; don't tempt it to arrive out of time. But neither is doubt the terrifying final word.

Doubt is sacred. Doubt is God's instrument, will arrive in God's time, and will come from unexpected places—places out of your control. And when it does, resist the fight-or-flight impulse. Pass through it—patiently, honestly, and courageously for however long it takes. True transformation takes time.

Being conscious of this process does not relieve the pain of doubt, but it may help circumnavigate our corrupted instinct, which is to fear doubt as the enemy to be slain. Rather, supported by people we trust not to judge us, we work on welcoming the process as a gift—which is hard to do when our entire life narrative is falling down around us. But we are learning in that season, as Qohelet did, to *trust* God *anyway* and not to trust our "correct" thinking about God.

Doubt is divine tough love. God means to have all of us, not just the surface, going-to-church, volunteering part. Not just the part people see, but the parts so buried no one sees them.

Not even us.

# Down the Mine Shaft

The dark places of the Bible—Psalms, Ecclesiastes, and Job—are valuable to us because they connect with the dark places of our souls. So let me say once again thank you to these parts of the Bible. You give us all permission to not fake it in our uh-oh moments.

But so many feel like they have to fake it.

They have heard sermons and lessons their whole lives where they were taught to think of the world in a certain "Christian" way, and then maybe in high school, maybe in college, they begin to see that life is more complicated and God doesn't work according to the plan. So a major disconnect rises up between what they had been taught and what they see. Their faith is no longer a convincing way of explaining the world, and so they leave it.

But we are pilgrims and have a lot in common with other pilgrims who also felt God's absence right in the Bible.

And then there's Jesus. On the cross, Jesus experienced the kind of dying we are talking about here and that is sure to come our way: God's abandonment—"My God, my God, why have you forsaken me?" (Matthew 27:46). No last-minute rescue. There couldn't be.

For Jesus, as for us, abandonment had to happen. Our periods of doubt, where God seems absent or in hiding, move us by God's grace further on in the journey, even when we may feel like we've left the path altogether. We are at that moment following the path that Jesus blazed.

Feeling abandoned by God may make us more like Jesus than when things are floating along swimmingly.

I first encountered this way of processing faith when I was introduced by some friends to the "dark night of the soul" and two sixteenth-century Spanish mystics, St. John of the Cross and his mentor Teresa of Ávila.

The dark night is the unrelenting sense of painful alienation and distance from God felt as distress, anxiety, discouragement, despair, and depression—and I've learned that it's a lot more common among us than we might feel comfortable admitting. Some experience this darkness more intensely than others, some for longer times than others. But the feeling is the same: they lose a sense of closeness to God and conclude that they no longer "have faith." And so they despair even more.

St. John's insight, which has meant a lot to me, is that the dark night is a special sign of God's presence. Our false god is being stripped away, and we are left empty—with none of the familiar ideas of God that we create to prop us up. The dark night takes away the background noise we have created in our lives in order to prepare us to hear God's voice later on—in God's time.

When the dark night comes upon us, we are being invited to surrender to God and trust him *anyway*. And, of course, this is very hard to do and leads us to why it's called a *dark* night in the first place: we have no control over what is happening. We all want to stay in control, especially people like me with the whole German type A personality thing going on. Darkness takes control away from us—which we hate.

I have several phobias. Here's one of them.

Imagine you're hiking along a wooded trail, and you come to an opening in the rocks—a mine shaft. You poke your head in and see a railroad car empty and resting on the tracks. You climb in to see what it feels like, which sounds like a good idea at the time—until your shifting weight nudges the car forward.

Before you even know what is happening, you're gathering speed. Within moments, the car is going too fast to jump out. Plus, now it's dark, and you can't see a thing. You're stuck and begin to panic. Where is this thing taking you? All you know is you're going down, you're probably going to die, and there's nothing you can do about it.

Soon you find that what you used to call "dark" gets even darker. You go on like this, faster and faster, deeper and deeper, for who knows how long, minutes that seem like hours. But then the slope begins to even out and the car slows before coming to an even stop.

You are now completely alone in a cave, far, far beneath the familiar surface. Probably thousands of feet down. All around you is a silence you never knew was possible, enough to hear the blood squishing through your veins. And it's so dark that the "pitch darkness" of even a secluded cabin would literally be a welcome sight.

You are completely disoriented. You have no sense of your surroundings—where the walls are, where the ground rises or falls. Unless you have the emotional capacity of a shrimp, you'd be scared out of your mind—maybe having a panic attack. "No problem, I got this; I'll just sit here and work this out" isn't part of your thinking process right now.

And finding a way out seems hopeless. You're just wondering whether you should risk moving at all. Eventually, you try to grope about on your knees, then take a few steps, gingerly at first, one way, then the other. Soon you realize that wherever you are, it's vast, dark, and flat, and you can't do anything about it. And you'd give an eye and a lung for a flashlight.

You are out of control. The dark controls *you*. That's what dark does.

Okay, that's a made-up story. Here's a real one—which changed my perspective on faith about as much as anything I can remember.

In 1975 the Jesuit philosopher John Kavanaugh went to work for three months at the Home for the Dying in Calcutta, India, with Mother Teresa. He was searching for an answer to his spiritual struggles. On his very first morning there, he met Mother Teresa.

"And what can I do for you?" she asked.

Kavanaugh asked her to pray for him.

"What do you want me to pray for?" she asked.

He answered with what I'm sure he felt was a perfectly reasonable and humble request, in fact the very reason for which he traveled thousands of miles to India in the first place: "Pray that I have clarity."

"No. I will not do that."

Kavanaugh asked her why.

"Clarity is the last thing you are clinging to and must let go of."

"But you always seem to have clarity."

Mother Teresa laughed. "I have never had clarity. What I have always had is trust. So I will pray that you trust God."

The first time I read this well-known story I was passing through my own loss of clarity, and God was a no-show in my life. I was like

John Kavanaugh—a "clinger," holding on to clarity so I could diagnose what the problem was, fix it, and move forward.

Wanting clarity is seeking some sort of control. A flashlight in the mine shaft. That's "all" I wanted. It doesn't even have to be on all the time. Just when I need it so I can get my bearings. I can handle this dark night, but on my terms.

But this is the dark night. No bearings for you. Then it wouldn't be dark anymore.

Darkness takes away control, what Thomas Keating and others call the "ego," that part of us that simply has to be in charge of our lives. That part that wants to cling to life, whereas Jesus says every part of us needs to die—especially the part that wants to retain control.

The darkness does us a favor by exposing control as an illusion. When everything is removed, "Where can I take back some control here?" eventually ceases being the active question and is replaced with a plea: "Lord, help me let go of control. Help me die. Help me trust."

That choice, it seems to me, sums up the life of Christian faith. And that is so very hard—and if anyone tells you Christianity is a crutch, you should take one of those crutches and beat him over the head with it (in Christian love, of course, making sure to tell them you will be praying for a quick recovery).

And you know, maybe that mine-shaft car doesn't come loose on its own. Maybe God nudges it a bit.

# Let's Bring This Aboveground

If you're guilt stricken because you harbor doubts and just can't seem to have your act together and be a happy Christian like your roommate or that lady in church, listen to Mother Teresa. According to her own journal, she was in her dark night more or less from 1948 until near the time of her death in 1997.

And all those noble and self-sacrificial things she did, things that may have made her one of the few public religious leaders who's never been the subject of an *SNL* skit or a *Daily Show* takedown. Perhaps her long dark night fueled her life, where she kept moving *anyway*, as an act of trust so deep it cannot be rationally explained—and indeed would look foolish if anyone tried. And the result was about as clear a Jesus movement as you can point to in recent history. Mother Teresa learned trust—not clarity, not certainty, but trust in God. And all of that poured out to the people around her.

I've heard it said many times: "Let go and let God." Or as the hymn says, "All to Jesus I surrender, all to him I freely give." But "letting go" and "surrendering all" might be more than we bargained for, and not something we can easily pull off on our own steam, nor might it even occur to us to try. Again, we're talking about a deep transformation, so deep it is described in the Bible as being nailed to a beam and left to suffocate slowly. And the self does not die quietly. We do not willingly go into the dark night.

When we are not letting go, when we try to stay in control of something—when we are "clinging" to something, as Mother Teresa said—perhaps that is when God mercifully turns off the light and makes it dark. Not because God is against us, but because God is for us.

When we are out of control, that is when God can speak to us—without all of the layers of God talk we have piled up inside of us. God puts us out of our control so that we can learn to trust rather than cling to knowing what we believe—a deeper state of being that the familiar meanings of *belief* and *faith* don't quite get to.

Trust.

Trust *is* letting go and learning to lean on God, and not our own insight, as we saw in Proverbs 3:5. Then we can get a taste at least of true liberation from our attachments, from our fears, and live with freedom and joy. That is the Christian journey. That is resurrection now.

One cannot have contentment in the Christian life without the darkness. Dying is the only path to resurrection, and that is the only way of knowing God. There is no shortcut. Jesus himself is our model for this.

When faith has no room for the benefit of doubt, then we are just left with religion, something that takes its place in our lives along with other things—like a job and a hobby.

Doubt is God's way of helping us not go there, though the road may be very hard and long.

# Cultivating a Habit of Trust

Deep calls to deep . . . all your waves and your billows have gone over me.

—Psalm 42:7

Do not let your hearts be troubled. Trust in God, trust also in me.

—adapted from John 14:1

# Ever Have One of Those Decades?

Me too. Mine was in the 2000s. My forties.

Life happened—quickly and often. It was a rough time, but I learned a lot about myself that I needed to learn, more than I ever thought I could know. I was beginning to see the difference between trusting God and controlling God in my thoughts.

To tell my story, I need to mention briefly the story of another, our daughter Elizabeth. Lizz's story is hers to tell, not mine, but she's allowed me to open that door to shed just enough light on how this one father, husband, and professor learned in his forties what he wished he had learned decades earlier.

Lizz had from day one been strong, extroverted, adventurous, cute as a button, and flat out spasm-inducing funny. Around the age of eight, however, she came to be fearful, unwilling to venture out and do the things she had always loved doing. In time, we all learned to give it a name: anxiety. The years that followed were difficult. Sue and I were winging it, pretty clueless about what anxiety was and how to address it.

Speaking now only for myself, my entire focus was on "fixing" my daughter. My intention was noble: I wanted to rescue her, but I only came to see years later that Lizz's battle with anxiety brought to the surface my own; by fixing Lizz, I was really trying to soothe myself. That dynamic only makes things worse for everyone, but I had no self-understanding about any of it.

I had been able to cover up my anxieties for most of my life, but when "life happens"—especially with your children—your world becomes chaotic and impossible to manage, like herding cats. Before you know it, you're overwhelmed. The long and short of it is that from the time Lizz was about eight until she was nearly seventeen, I was emotionally raw and walking on eggshells. Lizz's anxiety was not in my control, which made me more anxious, and round and round it went. It would take me years before I saw the toll that my thinking patterns took on me.

When Lizz was sixteen, her anxiety had become a lot more intense, and, among other things, she was in the early stages of an eating disorder. After a lot of searching, phone calls, and meetings, we eventually wound up making the hardest decision of our parenting lives. The best thing for Lizz was to get away from our family for a time. She would spend eight weeks in a therapeutic wilderness program in the hills of Georgia, and then go directly to a therapeutic boarding school in Arizona. Both were completely new concepts for us.

I actually felt relieved that Lizz would be in a setting where she could be helped. My hovering wasn't good for her, and it was harming me. On the other hand, sending your child to live in the woods without being able to monitor her (visits aren't allowed) was sad and fearful for both Sue and me. And then boarding school in Arizona?! Might as well be Siberia.

But those months away from home—sixteen in all—were healing for Lizz and for us. No one was fixed. In fact, during regular family therapy weekends in Arizona, the very idea of fixing other people was practically beaten out of me by some of the most compassionate and skilled people I ever met. And so we were all on a road to recovery. Things were looking up, and we were all encouraged.

By traveling such a difficult and lonely road and for so long, Lizz had gained tremendous spiritual insight. She experienced first-hand that when all you know of your life is ripped away from you—childlike trust in God is all you have, and it is enough.

I was happy for Lizz and relieved—for both of us. As far as I was concerned, Lizz was back and our troubles were behind us.

Not quite. I had no clue I was next on God's to-do list. I was about to take my own trip to Arizona.

# Live Strong

About a month before Lizz left for Georgia, I joined my son Erich's college baseball team on their spring training trip. As a lifelong Protestant, the baseball season was about the closest thing I had to a liturgical year, which begins for me, as it did for the ancient Israelites, in March (although mine doesn't involve a barley harvest).

And did I mention spring training was in Arizona?

I didn't know it at the time, but along with watching eight games in seven days, I was also scouting out the area where Lizz, in a few weeks' time, would begin a fourteen-month stay.

Before I left, Sue and I knew that Lizz would need to leave home very soon, and Lizz knew it, too. She asked me if I could bring home, of all things, a yellow Livestrong bracelet (long before Lance Armstrong's steroid scandal). I would have plenty of time to visit some malls, and this was at least *something* I could do to make Lizz feel better. But no luck. No one carried them, which seemed odd, since they were a "thing" at the time.

Lizz understood, but I so wanted her to have some symbol of strength. Even her asking for a symbol was a sign that she was determined to find a way to have courage and live her life.

Later that week, the players and their parents were at a poolside cookout hosted by two wonderful and generous college alumni. Being the congenial fellow I am, I struck up a conversation with our host, John, while he was flipping burgers. He stretched out his arm to reach for the seasoning, and on his wrist, what do I see two feet in front of me? Nothing other than the elusive yellow Livestrong bracelet—waving it like it was a banner.

I couldn't believe it. What a stroke of luck.

*I'll bet he knows where I can find one. Maybe . . . nah, that's crazy . . . but maybe he even has an extra one. That's stupid. Who carries extra yellow Livestrong bracelets?!*

But still, of all the possible strangers to meet in some random state I'd never been to, John was wearing the exact same bracelet I'd been seeking throughout greater Phoenix.

*I still have a couple of days left in Arizona, plenty of time to pick one up. He'll know where to get one.*

And even as I was processing that thought, I felt a chill up my back, a sense that something bigger was happening.

"Hey, you're wearing a Livestrong bracelet."

"Do you want one?"

(Momentary silence. I'm stunned.)

"I have a garbage bag of them inside. You can have a few."

A bag full. An abundance where my efforts had produced not a single one.

John answered a question I didn't ask. In fact, I didn't even ask a question.

By all appearances and in accordance with the accepted rules of social convention, I was simply making polite small talk: "Hey, love your cross-trainers. What year's your Volvo? When did you have your awesome grill put in?"

John should have responded in one of countless socially appropriate small-talk ways—"Yes, I'm a fan." "My friend has cancer, and I'm supporting him." "I've worn it for years." Something like that.

But instead, out of the blue, and without even a transitional comment—"Yeah, a friend of mine has cancer, so I wear it all the time. Say, do you want one? I've got a bunch left over from a fundraiser"—he just asked me, "Do you want one?"

Like he had heard a question where I only made a statement.

Like God was saying, "Move over, Enns. I'll ask him myself."

"Sure," was all I could bring myself to say.

I was an emotional wreck to begin with, but at this I had to turn away. I also felt my knees weaken, so I moved to a chair a few feet away and began to hold back tears. The party was going on all around me, and I was sitting there in my own world—in one of those surreal states where your periphery gets cloudy, like you're in a dream tunnel. *Did that just happen?*

A rubber bracelet. Such a dumb little thing. But I felt a Presence, and I "knew"—not in my mind, where I like to keep my knowing—but in my whole person, in defiance of my reason, that I was loved and remembered in the midst of my own fear and helplessness. I was overcome by hope, and glimpsed just enough to keep me going, that Lizz was not my problem to fix, that I had to let go of that very thought, and that I could trust God with my daughter. And as I came to see more clearly in time, this moment was simply an early step in unlearning control and cultivating a habit of trust.

I've thought a lot about that early evening in Arizona, but even as I write this, my inner skeptic tells me it was a coincidence, just one of those things that happens once in a while in a universe of infinite possibilities, and that my psycho-physical experience of a Presence was due to chemicals passing across neurons in my brain interpreted as a God moment. I also have a good idea what confirmation bias is—a tendency to search for or interpret information in a way that confirms one's preconceptions. My academic mind-set is tuned in to not accepting things at first glance—or at least knowing enough to feel guilty when I do.

And I've thought a lot about the selfishness of thinking that God showed up here for me at a cookout, yet religious extremists go from village to village killing, raping, and kidnapping, and God does nothing. I think of all those who responded to my survey, and how they might react if I dared interpret this as a God moment when they had been praying without ceasing for years with no relief.

But still.

I hear Aslan's words to Shasta: " 'Child,' said the Lion, 'I am telling you your story. . . . I tell no one any story but his own.' "

I don't *know* how it all fits together in the grand scheme of the universe. I can't explain it or be *certain* about what happened.

But, in a way, that's exactly the point.

Part of my own journey of faith is letting go of knowing *first,* of sorting it all out *first* before I commit. For me, a big part of learning to let go of knowing is to not care how or whether my experiences can fit together in some overarching intellectual structure where my rational mind remains enthroned as the true and final arbiter of what is and isn't real.

So I am just trying to tell my own story here, not anyone else's.

After nine years, I still can't shake that experience in Arizona, and recalling it now brings back those emotions, and I feel that feeling again. And I just can't shake the timing and the absurdity of that random exchange.

I have chosen to trust God enough to accept that this was a God moment that will always remain outside of my ability to comprehend or analyze. I embrace a different kind of knowing.

Probably for the first time in my life I was beginning to comprehend that trust was a habit I would need to cultivate. I was a seminary professor with a seminary degree and a Ph.D. in Old Testament. I was in my midforties with a wife and three teenagers. And it was time to learn to trust God. But that is my story. Don't judge me too harshly. Remember what Aslan said.

I took five bracelets from John. One for each of us. I kept mine on until long after Lizz came home from Arizona. Just so I would remember. It eventually got brittle and broke in half, but I've kept it on a dish next to my desk. Writing this reminds me to tape it together—and maybe to look at it more often. I need to keep my God moments before me.

# August 1, 2008

Along with a decade of stress at home, I was also facing a simultaneous and very serious stressor at work: my fourteen-year tenure as a seminary professor looked like it was coming to an end—at least some were determined to make it so.

Sticking with the bare storyline, several colleagues, some of them newly hired, had begun taking steps a year or so earlier to make sweeping changes in the composition of the faculty and administration, and those steps evolved into something of a well-orchestrated movement.

In the summer of 2005, I had published a book that reproduced more or less the content of what I had been teaching in my classes for twelve years with no sign of problems. But now, those views had become, for some, "controversial," meaning in violation of the school's ideological parameters. As a result, for almost three years I was viewed with suspicion, and regular faculty meetings were eventually held to "discuss" my work. With each passing month, the outcome became more and more self-evident: my days were numbered.

If you've ever been in a work environment where you face daily a concerted effort to put your head on a chopping block, but you have to go in day in and day out and sit in meetings with those who wish you weren't there and are exerting great effort to make it so, then you have a sense of what I was processing.

The inevitable loss of your livelihood is hard enough. But for me, home and work were coming unhinged at precisely the same time. And that was too much for me to handle—which I eventually came to realize was probably the point.

To pile it on, in the midst of all this, my father died, leaving my mother in a state that weighed heavily on me. A dear colleague, friend, and former teacher of mine also succumbed to a long illness a few weeks before Lizz left for Georgia.

Everything was happening in sync, with an unnerving rhythm and the precision of a Swiss watch. Waves of stress at work and at home were cresting and troughing at the very same moment. I recall some mornings having left the house in the middle of a true crisis, only to arrive at an office I didn't really want to go to in the first place and find waiting for me an e-mail or some rumor signaling the imminence of my professional demise.

And the crests weren't really crests. I was constantly under the waterline, just at different depths, never able to rest and catch a breath. I hardly came up for air. There were no even days, let alone good ones. Only variations on bad days. It seemed that stressors at home and work were collaborating, as if both worlds held morning staff meetings to get the timing right.

It was too much. I was completely drained—emotionally (Lexapro helped for a season), financially (wilderness and boarding school ain't cheap), and physically (I was stress eating and had put on some weight for the first time in my life). I was in new territory. A friend of mine genuinely wondered why I hadn't become an alcoholic.

My mom would tell me on the phone, "Peter, you have to give this to God. I mean *really give* this to God." But I wasn't ready to hear that just yet. I wasn't necessarily against the idea in theory, but trusting God seemed off topic at the time. I had begun learning to trust God with my daughter and family, but not with my own life. I needed to handle this myself, and right now, I was in survival mode. (Okay, *now* you may feel free to judge me.)

I wasn't yet self-aware enough to realize I was climbing into the car and about to head down the mine shaft.

After two years, it became clear to me (and many others) that no matter how many meetings we had or whatever other measures were attempted to call off the hounds, the scent of blood was in the air, and things would only get much worse. Rather than subjecting myself to a process with a foregone conclusion, I decided in January 2008—while Lizz was in Arizona—to take charge of the situation. After getting some sage advice, I contacted a lawyer and began moving toward a legal separation from the school I was once so proud of—the school that had educated me years before Lizz was born and had employed me since Lizz was in preschool.

This decision took a lot of the pressure off, but the next few months proved to be trying for other reasons. Although my intention to resign was known, a special board meeting was called for March where a vote was taken to suspend me. I was not there. My family and I were on a long-scheduled trip to visit Lizz in Arizona.

My case gained steam in the public eye (having been dubbed the "Enns controversy"), which added an element of shame further compounded by my feeling disparaged and misrepresented. Despite the majority of faculty supporting me, a carefully guided process was underway that I was helpless to stop. By May, after months of behind-the-scenes negotiations at my instigation, a severance agreement had been reached in principle.

Now the only thing that remained was working out the details back and forth and deciding on an official end date for my employment, which turned out to be August 1. It could easily (and more logically) have been earlier, July 1, the beginning of the fiscal year. But the process of ironing out details went slower than expected. Whatever.

During those months of negotiation, Lizz was also in the process of moving toward the end of her time in Arizona. Her school had no fixed graduation dates, since students enter at different times and go through the process at different paces. When a critical mass is reached, graduates are grouped together for one ceremony. So a lot of moving parts are in play, and it's hard to schedule graduation day more than a week or so in advance.

Early July came and went, and then mid-July, with tentative graduation dates scheduled in pencil and then erased. The date that finally worked turned out to be August 1. We marked it on our calendars and made the usual flight arrangements.

I didn't see the connection right away. My focus was 99.5 percent on bringing my daughter home after a long journey of healing, not on my job. But eventually, the beauty of it hit me. Lizz's difficult journey and mine, whose crests and troughs had been so exquisitely intertwined for years, were coming to an end—with a new life beginning on the exact same day.

Three hundred sixty-five days in a year, and two independent stories played out on opposite ends of the country, both converging in harmony on precisely one of those days. I felt like I did eighteen months earlier with John at his grill.

The convergence became more real for me as I sat there in Arizona, listening to Lizz give the valedictorian address. I was overcome by God's thick presence and a thankful heart—the kind of thankfulness that only comes by receiving grace rather than manufacturing it. Two hard journeys coming to an end in such alignment without—amazingly—my micromanaging a single moment of either. Go figure. I actually don't control the universe.

My family was being given permission to leave the past behind and move forward, though not as before, enslaved to fear, but by cultivating the seeds of trust that had been planted over the last few months.

# Honoring Your Head
# Without Living in It

When the Israelites defeated the Philistines at the town of Mizpah, the prophet Samuel set up a stone "between Mizpah and Jeshanah, and named it Ebenezer; for he said, 'Thus far the LORD has helped us'" (1 Samuel 7:12). You may know "Ebenezer" as Scrooge's first name, but in Hebrew, it means "stone of help," which Samuel placed at the battle site as a monument, a physical reminder of God's help.

We all need an Ebenezer or two in our lives. I know I do. Something we can point to.

As a boy (in middle school, if I remember correctly), I made myself a sandwich, tied together the bread bag, and tossed it back onto the counter a few feet away. My mother, who for much of her childhood in Poland and Germany during World War II had little to eat, looked at me with sad eyes.

"God cries when you throw food."

"I don't hear anything."

"You're not listening."

Maybe our Ebenezers are there and we need to listen better so we can recognize them. They may come softly, quietly, blended into our daily moments. And they may not come very often. But they may get us through long periods when remembering is all we have.

Our experiences of God matter—those sacred moments that defy the very rational capabilities we are so keen to rely on. And you know what? Throughout that time of struggle for me and my family, never was I preoccupied with lining up my thinking about God. There was no time for that, and it would have been out of place anyway. I was too busy surviving.

I had to let go—or better, the very idea of holding on was ripped from me. Like the guy in the mine shaft, trust was the only option available.

"You are of eternal worth." That's the message Lizz received in Arizona. Neither she nor I had ever heard that throughout our years of church life. And I began to wonder why. Instead, the starting point hadn't been our nonnegotiable humanity, but that we are deeply flawed and need to be fixed: pray more, do more, have more faith.

And I lamented, "Why did we never hear anyone say this in church?" It might have helped many build more healthy self-concepts—not in the superficial self-help sense. Our Arizona experience actually challenged us emotionally and *spiritually,* and our dysfunctional behavior patterns were laid bare in ways I had never remotely experienced in churches before. Speaking for myself, I felt more human, more whole, more honestly self-aware. And I didn't particularly like what I saw.

My theological training and "expertise" stood by silently watching it all happen. They had little to contribute that wasn't being handled quite well, thank you, by other means—a period of medication, family-systems therapy, individual therapy. Those things worked.

If we were so dramatically better off after a sixteen-month break from familiar Christian remedies, maybe my thinking about God, the world, and our place in it wasn't working very well. I found myself having to look at what I believed about God and God's actions in the world from an alien point of view.

This wasn't an academic exercise for me. I felt like pieces of my life were falling into place, and what I had always known about God wasn't fitting very well into this new scheme. I was at the beginning of a process of relearning how to "be" Christian—and becoming more spiritually self-aware than I had ever been. That process hasn't come to an end, and I see now that it never will. And I've come to see the wisdom of being fine with that—and trusting that God is, too.

I see my own life of faith as an ongoing rebuilding and renovation project. Though having passed official inspection, the flaws deep in the foundation have been exposed, as have the cracking walls and bursting pipes hidden behind them. Touch-up paint and caulk worked for a while, but they are at best temporary solutions—or worse, quick fixes that mask the cracks. Some walls have needed to be torn down and rebuilt with new framing, which has also given me the option to do some expanding and redesigning; the foundation of trust can handle it. I've expanded some rooms and rearranged others.

I still recognize my house as my own, even though it looks different from the street and has a different feel on the inside. And I know now that I need to make sure I don't let things go unchecked as I had before. Regular upkeep and vigilant maintenance are hard work and absolutely necessary.

Working on the lifelong habit of cultivating trust has meant learning to express my faith with words that rarely came to mind before—and that I might have mocked if they had—like *journey, pilgrimage,* and *mystery.* I know these ancient words of Christian wisdom can sometimes sound trendy and insincere, but not for me. They are my letting-go-of-control words. I've needed to be intentional in using different vocabulary not simply for describing my faith but for reconstructing it. The way we talk is not only a byproduct of how we think; vocabulary actually affects our mental architecture.

I made some friends who had already undergone a similar process of reconstructing their faith (some because of hard loss and excruciating pain). The quality of their lives of faith encouraged me, and they introduced me to extended communities of faith through writers I had either never heard of before or never took seriously enough to notice when correct thinking controlled my faith.

I know all this reading may sound a bit self-contradictory— reading books filled with information about needing to let go of holding on to information—but I don't see it as self-contradictory at all. As I've been saying, letting go of the need to be certain isn't the same thing as letting go of thinking. Reading outside of my comfort zone played a role in helping me understand that the need for certainty is at best a debilitating spiritual distraction, and at worst, simply destructive.

Discovering a contemplative tradition in Christianity was like opening a window in a dark room and seeing a crack of light that hinted at much more beyond. Here was a tradition for which mystery is not a slogan or reluctant concession but a deep, defining, and fundamental spiritual reality—a tradition, as I came to see, that went back even to the apostle Paul, who, as we saw, talks about being "in Christ," Christ being "in us," and our lives being "hidden" in God.

And in John's Gospel, we read that believers are as intimate with the Father and the Son as the Son is with the Father (John 17:20–25).

I never noticed this contemplative transrational dimension of the Christian faith because it was never taught. I felt a bit cheated, but I'm not sure if hearing about it years earlier would have helped. Not enough "life" had happened. Regardless, I now felt understood—which came at a pivotal moment in my life. For most of 2009 and 2010, God's absence was as profoundly tangible as was God's presence in Arizona two years earlier. Much like the writer of Psalm 73 or the writer of Ecclesiastes, and for the first time in my Christian life, I really wondered deeply whether it was worth it all, whether there actually was a God, and what it even means to speak like this.

I mourned that I might never be able to sing a Christmas song again, go to church, pray, or even care about any of that. I was between jobs and began looking for a new line of work altogether, but after many months of searching, nothing turned up. As I was bathing in my inner agnosticism, I was drawn to authors and others who were explicitly outside of the Christian tradition or not easily recognized as being in it—at least less easily than I had been accustomed to.

I felt I had to push myself to the outer edges of my known universe. After all, my old patterns of thinking had been disintegrated. Plus, if all this Jesus business is really real, he can handle it. And if he can't, well . . . whatever. But I'm not going to play around. That horse has left the stable. By peering out beyond my horizon, I got a different perspective on how inauthentic, carefully guarded, superficial, even fake, my own life of Christian faith had been, with its default mode of gaining knowledge to maintain my false sense of control at the expense of being aware of my own soul.

So it was huge for me to discover, in the midst of all this, an entire Christian tradition that confirmed my experience, which is when I began reading about the dark night of the soul—a cleansing acid bath to my preoccupation with correct thinking. My familiar pattern of needing to know now felt wholly out of place, even sacrilegious.

I was being led to a much bigger God—and a much more interesting and caring one.

I'm leaving out a lot of steps here; I'm not writing an autobiography. But I had a lot of periods of ups and downs, and still do. My point, though, is that these experiences have drawn me out of my safe haven of certainty and onto a path of trusting God—not trusting God *that* my thinking is correct or soon would be, but trusting God regardless of how certain I might feel.

My way of thinking was being tamed more severely than during those first moments at the Arizona barbeque. I was experiencing for myself what is really the point of this entire book: that trust means letting go of the *need* to know, of the *need* to be certain. And a long and honored Christian practice, diverse as it is, already existed that understood that process.

I also understood that the responsibility for where I had been and where I could go was all mine—a freeing and also unnerving thought. I was entering middle age, the "second half of life" as some call it, and was presented with the choice to remain where I had been or to press forward.

And somehow in the midst of all that, in a way I can't rightly quantify (and would cheapen it if I tried), I found myself becoming more conscious of God and the centrality of simple, uncluttered trust. I wish I could bottle that and write a bestselling "5 Steps" or

"50 Days" book, but I can't. At least for me, it doesn't work that way. Better, I don't think *God* works that way.

This is my process, not necessarily anyone else's. I'm not giving advice, another to-do list to give the impression of being in control of things.

I have also come to accept myself for what I am: I am wired as an explorer. I value challenging older orthodoxies and gaining new insights. That's neither good nor bad in and of itself. It just is what it is. I believe that I needed to learn to accept who I am, without apology, but also without falling into the trap of thinking that my particular type of faith, filled with books, languages, teaching, and writing, is the be-all and end-all of who God is. I was learning, and still am, to honor my head without living in it.

And a crucial part of all this was finding a flesh-and-blood community of faith that already modeled this expression of faith—and for me that wound up being a welcoming, Christ-centered Episcopal community.

I need to be in a place where the pulpit was off to the side and the table was central, symbols for me of letting go of old patterns, where lengthy sermons were the center of worship.

*I* need. Others may not.

I need Sunday morning centered on what is transrational, the fundamental Christian mysteries of incarnation and resurrection, the very heartbeat of Christian faith. Not irrational or unworthy of discussion and debate, but that which, when the intellectual dust has cleared, is ultimately beyond what our minds can grasp.

I need a God bigger than my arguments.

I like a prayer book and liturgy to guide me in my faith rather than falling back into my comfort zone of controlling reality with my learned and carefully chosen words, and without leaving it up to me to come up with what to say here and now when I just may not feel like it.

I teach, I write, I speak. All those words. I need to leave my words at home at least once a week.

I like reciting common words together with those sitting near me, with those far away, and with centuries of fellow pilgrims long gone. I need to be a part of something bigger than myself to believe with me—and when needed to believe for me.

I need a place to let go and fall back from my familiar patterns and trust God to catch me.

# The Long Haul

We've spent some time looking at the Old Testament—Psalms, Ecclesiastes, and Job—as we've been talking about struggling with faith, doubt, and the need to trust God whether or not our brains are keeping pace. The reason we've camped out in the Old Testament is because that is the part of the Bible that has the most to say about these things.

The Old Testament is a collection of writings written over a span of several hundred years. It comes to us from scribes, priests, royalty, and shepherds, writing in diverse times and places, under times of triumph and defeat. The Israelites had plenty of opportunity to have ups and downs, as a nation and as individuals.

One of the great comforts of Israel's epic is that it contains raw expressions of fierce doubt and lack of trust in God embraced by the ancient Israelites as *part of their faith*. I am thankful to God for *this* Bible rather than a sanitized one where spiritual struggles of the darkest kind are brushed aside as a problem to be fixed rather than accepted as part of the journey of faith.

The New Testament is different, though. It was written over

a much shorter period of time—probably about sixty years. Even though suffering is a key topic in the New Testament, the long haul of the Old Testament is not. In fact, the "end"—the return of Jesus—was thought to be right around the corner.

> When you see all these things, you know that he is near, at the very gates. Truly I tell you, this generation will not pass away until all these things have taken place.
> (Matthew 24:33–34)

> You turned to God from idols, to serve a living and true God, and to wait for his Son from heaven.
> (1 Thessalonians 1:9–10)

> Brothers and sisters, the appointed time has grown short. . . . The present form of this world is passing away.
> (1 Corinthians 7:29, 31)

> "Surely I am coming soon." Amen. Come, Lord Jesus!
> (Revelation 22:20)

Amid persecutions and other struggles that Christians endured, the tone of the New Testament writers was *urgency* to keep the faith because ultimate *triumph* is near at hand: "Hold on. It won't be long. Soon Jesus will return and God will set all things in order and your present sufferings will be over and justice will be served."

The problem we face today, of course, is that after two thousand years, the "end" hasn't come yet. And frankly, I don't know of many Christians who are gearing up for it. Most of us go about our lives without ever seriously thinking of stage two. I suppose we could go on living "as if" it were imminent, but it's hard shutting out the rest of life waiting by the door with your bags packed.

So here is my point: when it comes to living day in and day out in a messy world where things keep drudging on as they have been since forever and will continue on for the foreseeable future, the New Testament sense of urgency is hard to connect with.

In that respect, Christians today have more in common with the Israelites wandering through a lonely and threatening desert or exiled to a hostile land than with Paul and most other New Testament writers. The Old Testament doesn't speak in the booming voice of imminent triumph. It speaks of generation after generation of the faithful and not so faithful, of successes and failures, of God's presence and God's absence.

# Being Like Jesus

What then does the New Testament have to say about any of this? Plenty, but from a different angle altogether—an angle I'm going to go right ahead and call a mystical angle.

Paul doesn't call followers of Jesus "Christians." He calls them "in Christ." That isn't the easiest thing to understand, let alone explain, but it suggests an intimacy with Jesus that defies words.

That intimacy also includes—somehow—suffering.

When we cry out, "God, why have you forsaken me?" we are experiencing something of what Jesus experienced on the cross when he cries those same words (Matthew 27:46). The New Testament gets at this idea of suffering with Christ in different ways. For example,

> I am now rejoicing in my sufferings for your sake, and in my
> flesh I am completing what is lacking in Christ's afflictions
> for the sake of his body, that is, the church. (Colossians 1:24)

What exactly is "lacking" in Christ's afflictions and is "completed" by our suffering? I don't know, but it looks like our suffering intimately—mystically—connects us to Jesus's suffering in a powerful way and that benefits others.

Paul says that those led by the spirit of God are children of God.

And if children, then heirs, heirs of God and joint heirs with Christ—if, in fact, we suffer with him so that we may also be glorified with him. (Romans 8:17)

When reading Paul's letters, it's easy to get lost in the details, so let's not: suffering *with* (not for!) Christ is what children of God do. Suffering is not a sign that something is wrong with us and has to be corrected. Suffering is a key component of what identifies us as children of God.

And here is one of my favorite thoughts in all of Paul's letters:

I want to know Christ and the power of his resurrection and the sharing of his sufferings by becoming like him in his death, if somehow I may attain the resurrection from the dead. (Philippians 3:10–11)

Paul wants to "know" Christ, and (obviously) not in a "Hi, let's do lunch" sort of way.

Knowing Christ, for Paul, means not only experiencing "the power of his resurrection"—the triumphs and spiritual highs of the life of faith, the parts we can all quickly get on board with. It also means *necessarily* experiencing the dark times of the life of faith, the "sharing" of Christ's sufferings, participating in them, so to speak.

The two go together. Sharing Christ's suffering and death goes hand in hand with experiencing the power of Christ's resurrection.

In fact, suffering and death *necessarily* precede resurrection.

What is my point? The mystical language of "completing" Christ's sufferings, suffering "with" him, of "sharing" his sufferings, signals that suffering has some positive role to play in the life of faith, even if we can't grasp it well enough to understand it.

Of course, most of Western suffering doesn't involve prisons and tortures by violent regimes. But sufferings that are emotional and intellectual—like those laments of the psalmists, Job, and Qohelet—are no less true sufferings.

I am certain that Paul's suffering had to do with hostilities at the hands of the Romans and those who opposed his work. He may not have been thinking of faith crises like we have in our overly intellectualized modern Western world.

But that doesn't mean we can't see our faith crises as a form of suffering.

And I think we should.

Our psychological anguish over faith—sadness, despair, hopelessness, fear, worry—*is* suffering. The New Testament may not lay it out quite that way, but the Old Testament does.

So let me say it in a way that the ancient Israelites couldn't: *when we are in despair or fear and God is as far away from us as the most distant star in the universe, we are at that moment "with" Christ more than we know—and perhaps more than we ever have been—because when we suffer, we share in and complete Christ's sufferings.* And we don't have to understand that to know we should like it.

I am not glorifying suffering or papering over the pain. But when weariness and hopelessness settle in, at that very moment, our suffering is Christ's suffering and his is ours. We are more like Christ in these moments than we might realize.

Those times of despair, of not knowing how to put one foot in front of the other, of plummeting down a dark mine shaft of fear and despair, put us in a place where "correct" thinking is out of place. Only by laying down the need to understand and by accepting the mystery of faith can any of this truly make any "sense."

# Beyond Trust

Search me, O God, and know my heart; test me and
know my thoughts.

—Psalm 139:23

# No Fear

Letting go of the need for certainty is more than just a decision about how we think; it's a decision about how we want to live.

When the quest for finding and holding on to certainty is central to our faith, our lives are marked by traits we wouldn't normally value in others:

- unflappable dogmatic certainty
- vigilant monitoring of who's in and who's out
- preoccupation with winning debates and defending the faith
- privileging the finality of logical arguments
- conforming unquestionably to intellectual authorities and celebrities

A faith like that is in constant battle mode, like a cornered honey badger. Or like a watchman on the battlements scanning the horizon from sun up to sun down for any threat. And soon you forget what faith looks like when you're not fighting about it.

That kind of faith is not marked by trust in the Creator. It is stressful and anxiety laden, and it doesn't make for healthy relationships with others, including those closest to us.

On the surface, we might see here pride, arrogance, or belligerence, but those are simply symptoms of something deeper—a fear of being wrong and what might happen as a result.

But trust in God casts out fear and cultivates a life of trust that flourishes regardless of how certain we feel.

Trust is not marked by unflappable dogmatic certainty, but by embracing as a normal part of faith the steady line of mysteries and uncertainties that parade before our lives and seeing them as opportunities to trust more deeply.

Instead of relying on absolute either-or thinking, a trusting faith understands that trusting God is a process that takes time and practice. That pilgrimage doesn't necessarily follow a linear progression but accepts the unpredictable and disquieting nature of life as an encounter with God—and a move ultimately toward God, trusting that God is involved in that very process.

Rather than focusing on the badges that define our tribal identity (our church, denomination, subdenomination, doctrinal convictions, side of the aisle, whatever), a trust-centered faith will see the world with humble, open, and vulnerable eyes—and ourselves as members and participants rather than masters and conquerors. We will see our unfathomable cosmos and the people in our cosmic neighborhood as God's creation, not as objects for our own manipulation or unholy mischief.

Rather than being quick to settle on final answers to puzzling questions, a trust-centered faith will find time to formulate wise questions that respect the mystery of God and call upon God for the courage to sit in those questions for as long as necessary before seeking a way forward.

Rather than counting on the acquisition of knowledge to support and defend the faith, a trust-centered faith values and honors the wise—those who through experience and mature spiritual habits have earned the right to lead and are given a central role in nurturing faith in others.

Rather than defining faithfulness as absolute conformity to authority and tribal identity, a trust-centered faith will value in others the search for true human authenticity that may take them away from the familiar borders of their faith, while trusting God to be part of that process in ourselves and others, even those closest to us.

The choice of how we want to live is entirely ours.

# Go and Sin No More

Trusting God even when we can't or don't want to because nothing makes sense—especially then—is freedom, freedom from the pressure of needing to be certain when certainty has left us.

Choosing to trust the Creator then and there isn't irrational, but a humble admission that our rational faculties are limited for grasping the eternal and infinite. To call such trust irrational has already put on a pedestal the rationalistic pattern of faith that deeper faith calls us to transcend.

Trust acknowledges faith as transrational, submission to the mystery of the Spirit. For Christians, this is summed up in the mystery of a Creator who participates in the human drama. And all of this defies our analysis and the carefully sorted cubbies of our minds. Trusting this incarnating Creator gives us freedom to know or not know, to accept certainty when it comes or the absence of certainty, clarity or doubt, rest or restlessness.

Trust does not cancel our mind but circumscribes it and tames it—and so we do not succumb to fretting or anxious thoughts of being unsure.

I understand that the Christian faith is a long tradition deep in content. But pressing forward does not mean reproducing specific moments of that tradition from the good old days as if it were the best and permanent work of the Spirit. *"Do not say, 'Why were the former days better than these?' For it is not from wisdom that you ask this"* (Ecclesiastes 7:10).

I am a father and professor, and I get discouraged sometimes about the kind of faith we are passing on to future generations, where "protecting the past" is often goal number one. On one level I get it. But there is a difference, I believe, between a constructive respect for tradition and holding tightly to our image of God like an addiction—a Creator made in the worried image of created beings and to which we cling with a frenzied fury.

Rather than simply protecting the past, our faith communities have a sacred responsibility to protect the future by actively and intentionally creating a culture of trust in God, in order to deliver to our children and children's children a viable faith—

- a faith that remains open to the ever-moving Spirit and new possibilities, rather than chaining the Spirit to our past;
- a faith that welcomes opportunities to think critically and reflectively on how we think about God, the world, and our place in it, rather than resting at all costs on maintaining familiar certainties.

History has shown us that such a course adjustment wouldn't be the first time, or likely the last. In fact, we would simply be following the very template of scripture itself. The story of God and God's people is never static, never simply about repeating the past and maintaining it at all costs.

Israel's thinking about God was affected by its fifty years of captivity in Babylon in the sixth century BCE. Earlier, in the late seventh century, the prophet Nahum could write a scathing denunciation of the dreaded and super-mighty Assyrians and gloat over their deserved destruction by God's own hand (the capitol Nineveh fell in 612 BCE). But the book of Jonah, written sometime after the Israelites experienced the Babylonian exile (586–539 BCE), shows God commanding the prophet Jonah to preach repentance to the wicked Ninevites—to save them—much to Jonah's dismay.

Israel's faith was flexible, not set in stone.

Movement, change, and surprise are woven into the very fabric of the Christian faith. A crucified and risen Savior was the surprising act of God's faithfulness. It challenged conventional notions of what it meant for the God of Israel's story to show up—messiahs were supposed to rule from the throne in Jerusalem, not die. And this gospel continues to challenge our conceptions of God today.

A faith that remains open to God complicating our certainties will not only affect our own lives and the lives of those closest to us. It will also make us better world citizens.

Followers of Jesus throughout history have been of great service to the world in alleviating pain, suffering, and injustice. They have built countless schools, hospitals, and orphanages; have fed the hungry, clothed the naked, and housed the homeless; have worked tirelessly to protect the rights of the innocent and to abolish slavery. These acts are worthy of those who are called "the body of Christ" (1 Corinthians 12:12, 27), and the Bible speaks eloquently and repeatedly of justice and righteousness for the human family, of care for the widowed, orphaned, and strangers—the "others"—in our midst, of love that usurps self-glorification and power.

Yet, at least in my corner of the planet, Christians are often portrayed as syndicate thugs, known more for imposing eccentric certainties about science and morality on others. And so the gospel has become yet another calculating movement seeking power to impose on others its own version of divinely mandated order—another ideology claiming the divine stamp of approval added to the long list of such movements past and present that end in coercion, oppression, and violence.

The reputation Christianity has in the public arena has varied causes, to be sure, including our post-Christian culture, which has little use for religions of any sort. But ultimately some blame must fall squarely on the shoulders of Christian subcultures that are armed with an unwavering sense of certainty in what God wants here and now, which is not up for debate and must be imposed (to the glory of God).

Adopting and intentionally cultivating in Christians a culture of trust in God, rather than raising up soldiers for holy wars, would neutralize such public perceptions and reveal a bit more of the true Christian faith—and of God. Such a culture of openness to God's future is not a compromise to faith but a demonstration of it.

All this is to say that a faith in a living God that is preoccupied with certainty is sin, for it compromises the gospel—personally, locally, and globally. But it need not remain so. As Jesus said to the adulterous woman, *"Go your way, and from now on do not sin again"* (John 8:11).

Developing that culture of trust rather than preoccupation with certainty means discerning, articulating, and embodying the heart and soul of the Christian tradition, while also—and just as passionately—remaining open to the movement of God's Spirit, which *"blows where it chooses, and you hear the sound of it, but you do not know where it comes from or where it goes"* (John 3:8).

Faith like this does not come easily for many of us, and often it can only emerge at the tail end of difficult and trying experiences. For it is in those moments that we come to realize how little we actually know, that we have traded God for our own tired images of God, and that the frenzied pursuit of and clinging to correct thinking will sooner or later leave us empty and exhausted.

But if we venture further, we will then begin to see that trust in God, not correct thinking about God, is the beginning and end of faith, the only true and abiding path. Coming to this realization— for me as for others over the centuries—has made all the difference.

# Acknowledgments

This book is about faith, doubt, the wisdom of not needing to know, and learning that trusting God is the beginning, middle, and end of the Christian path. This book expresses that faith, and the faith to which I aspire.

I've been writing this book in my mind for about ten years, during which life transitions and just life in general were happening to my family and me with little time to come up for air. Actually, judging by an old journal I stumbled on from my early twenties, these themes have been my home base for over thirty years. I think I've always been writing this book.

Which explains why it took me a few tries to get this book looking like, well, a book, and not some random gushing of thoughts and stories with little focus. It took some time, but I eventually saw some themes and coherence amid the chaos, and *voila!* Here you go.

Many thanks to Mickey Maudlin, my editor, for his wisdom and insight into the Christian faith and what it means to write about it, and the rest of the team at HarperOne, who seem to have quite

213

a knack at seeing a book from draft to completion and beyond. It's great working with you.

Kathy Helmers, my agent, still believes in me, understands what I am trying to do, and seems to know where I am going before I get there. And I am likely the only person in human history who can say, "I played catch with my agent in November at an academic conference."

Spring Ridge Academy walked with us during a trying time and helped me see myself and my family more clearly. My friend Ted Olson picked up the slack and helped me to keep on seeing things more clearly. St. Matthew's Episcopal Church continues to refuse being wordy, trendy, flashy, loud, or caught up in culture wars.

Doug Green and Mike Kelly, friends and former colleagues, share a long and difficult journey with me. You are valued by many, including me, for who you are. Do not listen to those who only value you if you do as they say.

Gary and Maureen, you have lived the last few years with vulnerability amid pain—and you have introduced me and many others to the deeper catacombs of faith that I would not have seen otherwise.

Jackson Curreri, my student who read the proof pages, made sure I didn't do something truly stupid like confuse a citation from 1 Samuel with Galatians and other blunders I am prone to. David Vinson is a true friend, a brave and honest soul, and perhaps the fastest proofreader on the planet. Jared Byas, friend, coauthor, and collaborator, knows what I'm trying to do, sees implications long before I do, and doesn't hesitate to let me know when I'm veering off the path.

I would be remiss if I did not mention our house full of blissfully ill-trained animals. Marmalade, who is either purring on my lap or dutifully guarding (sprawled over) my keyboard, is singularly responsible for reducing my work efficiency by as much as one-third. Snowy, however, remains a very large and contagiously happy cat, whose only vice is needing to be fed hourly. Gizmo and Miley keep it real by lying around all day and barking at nothing. Newcomer and non-respecter-of-anyone's-personal space Stassi, the Italian Greyhound, draws the others out of their shells. And steady, contemplative Thumper more or less maintains his quiet routine of munching carrots and just sitting there.

And of course, my family:

Sue—teacher, masters student, writer, mother of our children, and dear wife of now thirty-one years—for your own courageous journey and for our journey together. Elizabeth Petters gave me permission to tell a small bit of her story in chapter 8. You and mom are the actual *writers* in the family. I just type a lot and hope for the best. Erich, an authentic and genuine spirit, with an uncluttered life and a no-nonsense pursuit for meaning. Sophie, a warrior dragon queen, honest, courage like steel, and compassionate.

Thanksgiving, 2015

# Notes

## Chapter 1: I Don't Know What I Believe Anymore

### Thanks for Nothing, Walt Disney

**Nothing looked remotely interesting except for Disney's film adaptation of *Bridge to Terabithia* . . .** The movie was released in 2007 and based on the book by Katherine Paterson published in 1977, which is now published by HarperCollins.

## Chapter 2: How We Got into This Mess

### Oh Great, We Came from Monkeys

**. . . in his famous . . . book *On the Origin of Species*.** Darwin's classic was published in 1859. The first edition sold out in a day. My copy is a facsimile of the first edition and published by Harvard University Press in 1964.

**. . . an evangelical Christian, Francis S. Collins, led an international team responsible for mapping the human genome . . .** Collins's first book on the subject is *The Language of God: A Scientist Presents Evidence for Belief.* Another helpful book of his, co-written with Karl W. Giberson, is *The Language of Science and Faith: Straight Answers to Genuine Questions.*

**. . . the earth isn't a few thousand years old, as the writers of the Bible likely assumed . . .** The age of the earth is commonly given to be about 4.5 billion year. According to Wikipedia's "Age of the Earth," the earth is 4.54 ± 0.05 billion years old.

**. . . the "known universe" is about 13.8 billion years old . . .** The numbers in this paragraph are based on *Wikipedia*'s "Speed of Light" and "Observable Universe."

## Seriously Weird Stories from Long Ago

**. . . when some curious archaeologists began digging in the Middle East . . .** Nineteenth-century British Egyptologist Flinders Petrie is considered the "father of modern archaeology." His systematic methods of excavating and dating artifacts quickly became the industry standard and led to greater understanding of the ancient Near East (aka, modern Middle East). Among the earliest finds to impact our understanding of the Bible was the Babylonian creation myth *Enuma Elish* (perhaps as early as the eighteenth century BCE). This story is similar to Genesis 1 at various points, which led scholars to begin looking at other parallels between the Bible and the older literature of ancient Israel's neighbors. I talk a bit more about *Enuma Elish* in chapter 3 of *The Bible Tells Me So*. Since the days of Petrie and the early stages of what would come to be known as "Biblical Archaeology," a lot of texts and artifacts have been discovered that help us place ancient Israel in its historical and cultural contexts. Scholars certainly debate particulars, sometimes with some intensity, but all agree that the "world of the Bible" has shed a lot of light on our understanding of the Bible.

## The Germans Are Coming (Like We Need This Right Now)

**. . . The Pentateuch . . . bears the marks of different writing styles . . .** Based on the work of other European scholars going back several generations, German Old Testament scholar Julius Wellhausen published his influential and controversial masterpiece *Prolegomena to the History of Ancient Israel* in 1882. Wellhausen argued that the Pentateuch is made up of four originally independent documents that were written between the tenth and sixth centuries BCE and then edited together in the fifth century, after the Babylonian Exile. Today most scholars question the details of Wellhausen's theory, but no scholar seriously questions the notion that the Pentateuch came to be over a long period of development—some might even say "evolution."

## Slavery: Whose Side Is God On?

**. . . the Bible itself gives conflicting information about slavery . . .** A great explanation of the crisis of biblical authority in the wake of the slavery issue is by Mark A. Noll, *The Civil War as a Theological Crisis.*

## Again with the Germans

**The only authority was "the natural light of reason" . . .** The phrase is that of radical philosopher, and no friend of organized religion, Baruch Spinoza (1632–77). He uses it throughout his famous work *Theological-Political Treatise* published in 1670. A contemporary version is *Spinoza: Theological-Political Treatise,* edited by Jonathan Israel.

**Luther's Germany, and elsewhere in Europe, is also where modern biblical scholarship would take root within two hundred years . . .** Luther's call to reform the Church had unintended consequences. The whole matter is involved and hard to capture in a few sentences. An excellent (though expensive and academic, yet readable) source is *Spinoza and the Rise of Historical Criticism of the Bible* by Travis L. Frampton (T&T Clark, 2006). The key chapter is chapter 2, "Protestantism and the Historical Sense of Scripture." For example, in his debates with the Catholic hierarchy, Luther appealed to Scripture and "plain reason" to defend his views—which is precisely the rhetoric used by later more radical figures like Spinoza.

## Why "Defenders of the Faith" Are Raising White Flags

**. . . they share the *same starting point* . . .** Recent decades of biblical scholars and theologians have called into question the entire modern intellectual project, with its confidence in being able to give certain, objective knowledge about the nature of reality, past and present. Two great critiques of modernity by biblical scholars are Walter Brueggemann's *Texts Under Negotiation* and Walter Wink's *The Bible in Human Transformation.*

# Chapter 3: "You Abandoned Me, God; You Lied" (and Other Bible Lessons)

## Parts of the Bible We Don't Read in Church (but Should)

**The 150 Psalms we have in our Bible are basically of three types . . .** In terms of their *mood*, the Psalms can be divided as I have it here. But biblical scholars spill a lot of ink laying out in great detail the various types of psalms you encounter in the book of Psalms. Scholars don't agree entirely on what those categories are and they don't always use the same vocabulary, but, if you look at any book introducing the Psalms (like Bernard Anderson's *Out of the Depths*), or just a decent study Bible (like *The New Interpreter's Study Bible*, *The HarperCollins Study Bible*, or *The Jewish Study Bible*), you read about a wide variety of psalms. Some psalms are sung by individuals and others by the whole community. We see psalms of thanksgiving, praise, complaint, lament, and petition, along with wisdom psalms, royal psalms, and processional liturgies. The book of Psalms is a beautifully diverse collection of ancient Israel's songs of worship and faith.

**Walter Brueggemann calls these parts of the Bible Israel's "countertestimony" . . .** This spot-on term to name the dark side of the Bible, and which calls into question Israel's main storyline, comes from Walter Brueggemann's *Theology of the Old Testament: Testimony, Dispute, Advocacy*.

## The World Makes Perfect Sense Without God

**. . . "Grace grows best in winter" . . .** The quote is from Samuel Rutherford's "Letter 74 to Lady Culross Aberdeen 1837" in *The Letters of Samuel Rutherford*.

# Chapter 4: Two Miserable People Worth Listening To

## Trust God Anyway

**. . . the main speaker of the book, the otherwise unknown Qohelet . . .** The name Qohelet comes from the Hebrew verb *qahal*—to "assemble"—which suggests Qohelet is a "leader of an assembly," a far better option than interpreting the name as "Teacher" or "Preacher." Still, leaving the name as is seems best. Qohelet is a fictitious figure, a literary persona, styled as a king, and as such bears the theological message of the book's author. I discuss all this in my commentary, cleverly titled *Ecclesiastes*.

## Don't Even *Try* to Understand What God Is Up To

**He stands firm in his effort to get an answer from Yahweh.** The last words of Job (42:1–6) are routinely understood as Job humbling himself before God and acquiescing to God's power, especially v. 6. The meaning of this verse is debated (what isn't among biblical scholars!), but commentaries and study Bibles lay out the problems with this conventional interpretation. To some interpreters, Job is anything but turning over and playing dead. Long story short, Job is mimicking God in the first few verses, and v. 6 is not a moment of repentance but Job holding his ground: "I reject and regret dust and ashes" (*The New Interpreter's Study Bible*) or "I am disgusted and take pity on wretched humanity" (*The Jewish Study Bible*). Job is not humbling himself before God and crying "uncle." He is resigning himself to the fact that God is never going to give him a straight answer.

## Chapter 5: Believing in God: So Easy Even a Demon Can Do it

### Faith Isn't Something in Your Head (or Heart)

**. . . the Greek word behind it is the same one translated as "faith" elsewhere in the Bible: *pistis* (PIS-tis).** That is not quite right. *Pistis* is the noun, and can mean belief or faith. There is also a verbal form of the word, *pisteuo* (pis-TYOO-o). Since faith is not a verb in English (we don't "faith" something), translators use a different word ("believe") or add the helping verb "have faith," both of which can confuse things and fall short of getting at what these words convey, as we see in this chapter.

**A better reading is "*faithfulness of* Jesus Christ" . . .** This way of understanding Paul in Galatians 2:16 has gained a lot of support in recent decades, due to a better understanding of Paul's letters as a whole. Paul's letters focus not so much on communicating a set of beliefs that will lead you to heaven when you die. Instead, Paul's focus is on how God has made Jews and Gentiles one people of God through the death and resurrection of Christ. This may seem like a bit of a letdown for some of us, but Paul's message (Paul's "gospel" as he calls it)—that Jesus is the messiah of Israel, who was crucified and raised from the dead, and that Jesus was messiah equally for both Jews and Gentiles—was a huge crowd control problem for Paul. As Gentiles began following this Jewish messiah, Jewish followers of Jesus rightly assumed that these newcomers would need to adopt certain longstanding Jewish practices commanded in the Bible, namely circumcision and dietary laws. These practices, which Paul refers to as "works of the law" in Galatians 2:16 and elsewhere, were "identity markers" to mark one off as Jewish in Roman society, and it was assumed Gentiles would join right in. But Paul argued that these practices, however ancient and biblical they may be, no longer mark one off as the people of God—no longer "works of the law" but rather what Jesus has done (Jesus's faithfulness), in whom we now place our trust (our faith). Disagreement over whether these Jewish practices remained valid and binding threatened to tear apart this fledgling community of Jesus followers, and if it did, it would be seen as proof that the gospel doesn't work and therefore isn't true. Holding together this disparate group of believers was a prime focus of Paul. The debate whether we should read "faith in Jesus Christ" or "faithfulness of Jesus Christ" is in full swing today, with scholars arguing for one, the other, or some point in between. Books and articles could fill a small library, and any decent commentary written in the past thirty years is sure to mention it. One of the more readable books is N. T. Wright's *Justification: God's Plan and Paul's Vision* or *What Paul Really Said*.

## There Goes Jesus Being Jesus Again

**Thomas Merton's well-known prayer . . .** An honest prayer loved by many for having its finger on the pulse of the struggles with faith. See Thomas Merton's *Thoughts in Solitude*.

## But, But . . . What About . . . ?

**The Bible is a book of diverse voices that speaks into diverse situations . . .** This issue is one of the main themes in *The Bible Tells Me So*. The writings that eventually made up the Bible (both testaments) were written over a wide span of time—about 1,000 years—by people in diverse and challenging historical and personal situations. They do not all speak with one voice, nor should we expect them to. Plus, neither scribes who edited Israel's scripture after the Babylonian

Exile nor the Christians who compiled the New Testament between the second and fourth centuries CE seemed to be particularly concerned about cleaning up the diversity.

## Chapter 6: Uh-Oh: When Certainty Is Caught Off Guard (and Why That Might Not Be Such a Bad Idea)

### When Life Happens

**These are questions I asked on a survey . . .** You can find this survey in the post "5 Main Challenges to Staying Christian, and Moving Forward Anyway" on my blog, *The Bible for Normal People,* at www.peteenns.com.

### God Did *What,* Now?

**High on the list of violent acts was God's command that the Israelites enter Canaan . . .** I look at biblical violence, especially God's command to exterminate the Canaanites, in more detail in chapter 2 of *The Bible Tells Me So.* I also talk there about how these stories of violence mirror how ancient tribal cultures saw the gods. The flood, massacre of Canaanites, and other such acts of violence don't tell us what God is like but how the Israelites, an ancient tribal people, understood and worshiped God. Readers today are not meant to think of God the same way, because the Bible is not a handy information packet on God from A-Z but a record of Israel's understanding of God, often penetrating and consoling, but also incomplete and disturbing.

### Our Pale Blue Dot

**. . . the immeasurably vast size of the universe.** See notes in chapter 2 regarding *Wikipedia*'s "Speed of Light" and "Observable Universe." Rob Bell has a great section in *What We Talk About When We Talk about God* (chapter 2, "Open"). He looks at the role science has played in showing us how mysterious and unknown our universe becomes the more we learn about it; for example, subatomic particles disappear and show up instantly elsewhere, and space-time isn't constant, but warps. Science pushes us to accept mystery rather than dismiss it.

**Seventeenth-century philosopher Blaise Pascal . . .** Blaise Pascal, "Of the Necessity of the Wager" sec. 3, no. 206 in *Pascal's Pensées.* Thought (*Pensée*) number 205 is also worth looking at: "When I consider the short duration of my life, swallowed up in the eternity before and after, the little space which I fill, and even can see, engulfed in the infinite immensity of spaces of which I am ignorant, and which know me not, I am frightened, and am astonished at being here rather than there; for there is no reason why here rather than there, why now rather than then. Who has put me here? By whose order and direction have this place and time been allotted to me?" Blaise Pascal, meet Qohelet!

**Our home planet, as Carl Sagan put it, is a "pale blue dot" . . .** The "Pale Blue Dot" is a moving soliloquy by Carl Sagan in his 1980 television series *Cosmos.* The remake of this series, which aired in 2014 and was hosted by Neil deGrasse Tyson, replayed Sagan's soliloquy toward the end of the final episode (episode 13, "Unafraid of the Dark") with stunning graphics to illustrate that the Earth is a "mote of dust suspended in a sunbeam."

**Humans have been around for a long time, doing humanlike things . . .** The examples in this and the next paragraph are taken from Andrew Curry's November 2008 *Smithsonian Magazine* article "Göbekli Tepe: The World's First Temple?" and *Wikipedia's* "History of Wrestling," "History of Beer," and "Stonehenge."

**Are we, then, as "neurotheologians" put it, simply a mass of chemicals and neurons . . .** *Wikipedia* describes "Neurotheology" as "a neologism that describes the scientific study of the neural correlates of religious or spiritual beliefs and practices. Other researchers have rejected the term, preferring to use terms like 'spiritual neuroscience' or 'neuroscience of religion.' Researchers in the field attempt to explain the neurological basis for religious experiences, such as: the perception that time, fear or self-consciousness have dissolved; spiritual awe; oneness with the universe; ecstatic trance; sudden enlightenment; altered states of consciousness."

## Falling Branches

**While jogging along a wooded trail in an area park . . .** My two illustrations were reported by *ABC Philadelphia* ("Woman Killed by Tree Branch Identified") in 2009 and *NBC Philadelphia* ("5-Year-Old Boy Dies After Tree Falls on Him in Montgomery Country") in 2012.

## God Is Not My Father

**. . . like the parts where God actually does love the world and has nurturing patience like a mother . . .** On God's love, see John 3:16 and 1 John 4:8. On God like a nurturing mother, see Isaiah 49:15 and Psalm 131:2.

## When "Uh-Oh" Becomes "Ah-Ha"

**Adjusting our expectations about what the Bible can deliver . . .** This is a major, if not *the* major, theme in *The Bible Tells Me So.* Having false expectations about the Bible is the biggest "crisis" over the Bible that we face.

# Chapter 7: God Wants You Dead

## The Lie: "It's All Your Fault"

**Doubt—not fashionable skepticism, but really doubting what you were always so certain of . . .** It seems to me that in recent years, more and more authors are writing about the role of doubt in the Christian Life—and they are clearly hitting a raw nerve. To mention just a few: Brian McLaren, *The Last Word and After That*; Valerie Tarico, *Trusting Doubt*; Greg Boyd, *Benefit of the Doubt*; Rachel Held Evans, *Faith Unraveled* (formerly, *Evolving in Monkeytown*); Philip Yancey, *Disappointment with God*; Anne Lamott, *Plan B: Further Thoughts on Faith*.

## Down the Mine Shaft

**. . . two sixteenth-century Spanish mystics, St. John of the Cross and his mentor Teresa of Ávila.** Gerald G. May's *The Dark Night of the Soul* was my great introduction to John of the Cross and Teresa of Ávila.

**In 1975 the Jesuit philosopher John Kavanaugh . . .** For the dialogue between Kavanaugh and Mother Teresa, see Brennan Manning's *Ruthless Trust*. An account of Mother Teresa's journey in a collection of her letters is *Mother Teresa: Come Be My Light* (edited by Brian Kolodiejchuk). The name of the home has since been changed to "Home of the Pure Heart" as has the name of the city to Kolkata.

**Darkness takes away control, what Thomas Keating and others call the "ego,"** . . . Thomas Keating is a Trappist monk and priest whose work in the 1970's revived the contemplative tradition in Roman Catholicism. *Invitation to Love* is a good introduction to this moment.

## Chapter 8: Cultivating a Habit of Trust

### Ever Have One of Those Decades?

**To tell my story, I need to mention briefly the story of another** . . . As I said, Lizz's story is hers to tell—and she is. She blogs regularly (under Elizabeth Petters) out of her deep experience on faith, living in the moment, and trusting God.

### Live Strong

**I hear Aslan's words to Shasta** . . . The scene is Shasta asking Aslan why he had earlier wounded Aravis in C. S. Lewis's *The Horse and His Boy*. I can't tell you how much the Chronicles of Narnia series meant to me when I first read them *after college*!! And they still mean a lot to me.

### August 1, 2008

**I was also facing a simultaneous and very serious stressor at work** . . . In this section I recall briefly my departure from Westminster Theological Seminary in 2008. The focus of the "controversy" was the publication of *Inspiration and Incarnation*. The matter became quite public, landing me on the cover of the *Philadelphia Inquirer* ("Embattled Professor to Leave Seminary") and attracting the attention of the local NPR station (resulting in a WHYY's *Radio Times* interview with Marty Moss-Coane). Good times.

### Honoring Your Head Without Living in It

**. . . they introduced me to extended communities of faith through writers I had never heard of before** . . . Along with the writings of Gerald May and Thomas Keating, whom I had not known before, I was encouraged to explore or revisit a few other writers, including Richard Rohr (*Adam's Return* and *The Naked Now*), Thomas Merton (*Thoughts in Solitude*; also James Martin's introduction to Merton and others, *Becoming Who You Are*), Henri Nouwen (*The Inner Voice of Love*), Gregory Mayers (*Listen to the Desert*), Rowan Williams (*Tokens of Trust*), J. Keith Miller (*Compelled to Control*) and David Benner (*Spirituality and the Awakening Self*). Let me also include here Frederica Matthews-Green (*The Jesus Prayer* and *At the Corner of East and Now*) for gentle and compelling introductions to Eastern Orthodoxy, a direction to which I never once nodded throughout my entire seminary career, and James Fowler's classic *Stages of Faith*. Others I want to mention are M. Holmes Hartshorne (*The Faith to Doubt*) and Daniel Taylor (*The Myth of Certainty* and *The Skeptical Believer*). I could go on, but each of these were one ah-ha moment after another, encouraging in me a different perspective on what the life of faith can look like, which I found both unsettling and also healing and freeing. These books have become old friends.

**I was drawn to authors and others who were explicitly outside of the Christian tradition . . .** Such as Joseph Campbell (*The Power of Myth*), Robert Bly (*Iron John*), Don Miguel Ruiz (*The Four Agreements*), and Sam Keen (*Fire in the Belly*). I also re-read Viktor Frankl's classic *Man's Search for Meaning* (which my daughter Lizz and my wife Sue also read while Lizz was away).

**I was entering middle age, the "second half of life" . . .** I need to mention here again Richard Rohr (first through podcasts and then *Falling Upward*), along with James Hollis (*Finding Meaning in the Second Half of Life*).

## The Long Haul

**. . . after two thousand years, the "end" hasn't come yet . . .** For an alternate and provocative understanding of Jesus's second coming, see the many posts by Andrew Perriman at "P.OST" (postnost.net). He argues that the second coming is best understood within the conceptual framework of the Bible. That means that these events were fulfilled politically: the destruction of Jerusalem, the dispersion and formation of Christ communities throughout the Roman Empire, and ultimately the overthrow of pagan Rome and the confession of Christ as king by that empire. This brings about an end to persecution of faithful Israel and the worship of Israel's God among disparate nations. Whether or not you find this convincing, the church is still in the long haul, nevertheless, as was ancient Israel and its successor, Judaism.

# Chapter 9: Beyond Trust

## Go and Sin No More

**The story of God and God's people is never static . . .** A wonderful book that got me started in thinking about this is Paul Hanson's *Dynamic Transcendence: The Correlation of Confessional Heritage and Contemporary Experience in a Biblical Model of Divine Activity.* He speaks of a "form-reform" dynamic in the Bible. The law is a classic example in the Old Testament. Law was given in conjunction with Israel's liberation from slavery—it was not a burden, but a mark of freedom and a covenant bond with God. Yet, that form became institutionalized over time to mere ritual. The prophets spoke to this ("I desire steadfast love and not sacrifice . . ."; Hosea 6:6). Jesus in the Sermon on the Mount had a similar vibe ("You have heard that it was said [in the Law of Moses] . . . but I say to you . . ."; several times in Matthew 5 beginning at 5:21). And with the prophets as with Jesus, it was the gatekeepers that resisted reform—those with much invested in maintaining older forms at all costs. This "form-reform" pattern, Hanson argues, has also been played out throughout the history of Christianity—it seems unavoidable. The pattern of reforming earlier views that become encrusted with rote tradition is not a regrettable situation to be avoided, but a means of insuring a continued deep fidelity to the heart—not the letter—of any faith tradition.

**Earlier, in the late seventh century, the prophet Nahum could write a scathing denunciation . . .** The dates I give here for Nahum and Jonah are uncontroversial among biblical scholars. Jonah was written sometime during the Persian period—which ruled from modern day India all the way to Egypt and Asia Minor after dismantling the Babylon Empire in 539 BCE and until the rise of the Greeks in 332 BCE. Nahum is dated to some time in the middle to late seventh century BCE, near the time of the fall of Assyria's capital Ninevah in 612 BCE.

# Scripture Index